AF267716

To all the places I've been and those I've yet to go.
To all the people I've met and those still waiting on the path ahead.
To all the lessons I've learned and the ones still to come.
To this life I'm grateful for and the life I dare to dream about.

This memoir is my love letter to you.

To the dreamers who are also realists.
The humorists who are also healers.
The travelers, thinkers, feelers, and fighters.

May your world be graced with just enough beauty to keep you tender,
just enough truth to keep you honest,
and just enough laughter to carry you through the storm.

To Nanay —

I miss you.

Copyright © 2026 by Novie Onor

Published by ONOR Press
An imprint of Onor Advisory Pty Ltd, Australia

All rights reserved.

No part of this publication may be reproduced, stored in a retrieval system, or transmitted in any form or by any means (electronic, mechanical, photocopying, recording, or otherwise) without the prior written permission of the author, except for brief quotations used in reviews, scholarly works, or critical articles.

This is a work of nonfiction. Some names and identifying details have been changed to protect the privacy of individuals. Any resemblance to real persons, living or dead, is purely coincidental unless explicitly stated.

Cover design, interior layout, and formatting by the author.

Published in Sydney, Australia.

For permissions, speaking engagements, or correspondence, please email:
novie@onoradvisory.com | novie@onorimmigrationlaw.com

www.onoradvisory.com | www.onorimmigrationlaw.com

First Edition
ISBN: 978-1-7646151-0-5

Advance Praise for

Noble and Honorable Adventures:
Lessons in Identity, Courage, and Becoming

"Inspiring, powerful, and profoundly moving. A narrative that makes the soul feel seen." — Kitt (Philippines/Greece)

"Delightful, original, and heartfelt. A slow-burn unveiling of a fascinating life." — Mark (Australia)

"A modern-day José Rizal in prose. A literary feast for anyone living between worlds." — Jean (Philippines/Australia)

"More than a memoir, it's a lifeline of hope for anyone chasing dreams across borders." — Lin-Chu (Taiwan/Australia)

"Courageous, vivid, and compelling. A story with the power to resonate." — Hana (Algeria/Germany)

"Witty, heartfelt, and rooted in gratitude. A story that lingers long after the last page." — Lui (Philippines/France)

"Revelation and inspiration. Proof that with courage, anything is possible." — Karla (Philippines)

"Resonant, wise, and unforgettable. A migrant's journey told with clarity and heart." — Julian (Philippines/Australia)

"An enlightening book filled with lines you'll want to highlight and carry with you through life's challenges." — Geraldine (Philippines/United States)

CONTENTS

PART III: BECOMING

Before You Begin
(Or: Why This Book Isn't Just a Memoir)

Noble and Honorable Adventures sounds like a medieval quest or something involving armor. But really, it's about adventure that doesn't look heroic from the outside. Folding hospital corners, learning to pronounce *jurisprudence* with a Filipino accent, and emailing strangers to prove you belong.

Noble, because there's dignity in striving, even when you don't feel seen.
Honorable, because doing the right thing, even when it's hard, unpaid, or unrecognized, still counts.
Adventures, because becoming yourself across countries, careers, and crises is nothing short of epic.

You'll notice three words beneath the title:
Identity, Courage, and Becoming.
They're not just chapter themes. They're the arc.

Identity is the soil. Not just where you're from, but how it shaped how you dream.
Courage is the wind — the decision to keep going when you're tired, out of your depth, or the only one in the room who knows where Mindanao is.
Becoming is the sky — not a destination, but an unfolding horizon.

This memoir isn't a gallery of polished trophies, but a constellation of small, trembling stars. Imperfect, radiant, stubborn in their becoming.

It's less a highlight reel than a blooper reel with a heartbeat. It's full of missteps that somehow made progress.

Not a memoir of a finished man, but a mirror to the mess and meaning we all navigate.

It isn't a purist literary memoir. It isn't a preachy self-help manual either. It lives somewhere *in between*. Much like me. Unboxed, borderless, and better for it.

If you're here for literature, I hope you'll find lines that linger, rhythms that hum beneath the words. I didn't study under professors with linen shirts or surrounded by first editions of Nabokov. But I've read enough to know what moves me. Enough to know that the books that stayed with me weren't trying to sound wise. They were being *honest*.

I didn't come from the land of Hemingway.
I come from the land of Manny Pacquiao.
Which is to say: I grew up not with a pen in hand, but grit in my bones. English wasn't my first language. Storytelling came later.

And yet here I am.

These chapters weren't written in a retreat. They were carved out of real life. Between nursing shifts and case files, across time zones, and in the fog between survival and self-discovery.

So no, this may not sound like your usual literary debut.
But perhaps that's the point.

I respect literature. I just didn't want to imitate anyone. At times, this memoir will break convention. I'll speak to you, the reader. I'll italicize non-English words. Not to *'other'* them, but to honor them. To preserve their cultural soul.
(If you're ever curious, there's a glossary at the back.)

And if you came looking for honesty over polish, I hope you find that too. This memoir is not a tidy narrative. There are no neat epiphanies or foolproof frameworks. Just a few stories. Some hard-won grace. And perhaps a mirror you'll catch yourself in.

There's a chapter about France. Long walks, slow beauty, borrowed books, and questions I didn't yet have answers to. Then there's Germany, where I worked, earned, structured, kept my visa valid. Learned to become useful in ways that weren't always romantic but were necessary.

This memoir moves like that too. Between reflection and responsibility, between meaning and momentum. Not in contradiction, but in conversation. Because sometimes beauty builds you, and sometimes structure does. And sometimes, if you're lucky, they meet in the same story.

Inside, you'll find stories about selling *yema* to pay for debate tournaments. About warming leftovers in hospital break rooms while memorizing case law and running between airports and deadlines, chasing both visas and voice.

This memoir honors the Filipino heritage, the Australian experience, the European journey, the American dream, but it isn't written for any single passport. It's written for the human heart.

You'll find chapters carved from call bells and courtrooms. Not a roadmap to success, but a glimpse into the hard work of human hands.

There are cultural collisions. Parisian classrooms, German law firms, Australian ICUs, and family calls that begin with *"Have you eaten?"*

Some moments feel cinematic. Others smell like reheated rice and bureaucratic fatigue. There's humor, too. Dry, mostly, but earned. The kind that sneaks in after grief, or during it.

And in between the visa queues and clinical corridors, there are glimpses of wilderness. Hiking through New Zealand's Great Walks — Kepler, Tongariro, Routeburn — with nothing but a borrowed backpack, questionable map-reading skills, and too many thoughts. Not just trails but turning points. Places where I stopped trying to outrun burnout and learned to be still.

Because this isn't just a memoir about movement. It's also about what happens when you finally pause long enough to hear your life speak back.

Each chapter ends with a reflective prompt. Not a task, just a nudge. Skip them, scribble on them, or sit with them. Whatever you need.

I've called them **Soul Notes** — not because they're profound, but because they're personal. They're not here to instruct, but to invite. Think of them as postcards to your inner life. Soft landings for your memories, meanings, and truths.

So if you've ever lived between versions of yourself, or wondered if all the effort is building toward something that matters —

If you're chasing a dream that keeps slipping just out of reach, or carrying a restlessness you can't name —

If you've built a life on resilience, but still wonder when the ease begins, or if it ever does —

If you've ever tried to become something, or someone —

If you're simply looking for something honest to hold onto for a little while —

This is for you.

Not a perfect guide. Just a steady companion.

A reminder that some of the most noble and honorable adventures don't look epic. Many are human, but worthy, nonetheless.

This isn't just my story. It's *ours*.

Prologue: My Noble and Honorable Adventure

Most people think a good life follows an arc: study hard, work smart, achieve success, then, if you're lucky, reflect.

Mine never followed that arc. It zigzagged. Fast. Across countries and careers, constantly in motion.

And somewhere in the rush, I wondered:
Was I building a life? Or just a case for why I deserved to exist in one?

I've lived several lives in one:
> — registered nurse in the Philippines, New Zealand, Australia, and the U.S.
> — licensed attorney in Australia and New York.

That means I can check your visa paperwork *and* your blood pressure, usually in the same conversation.

I've been a legal scholar in France. An Olympic volunteer. A migrant. An immigrant. A serial test-taker, visa-holder, and border-crossing shapeshifter.

I've crossed oceans. Passed boards. Earned degrees.

I've skydived in Queenstown and Hawaii, eaten the best tiramisù in Rome, and stood at the top of the Eiffel Tower. It probably sounds impressive. Perhaps it is. But that's never been the whole story.

I've done things that many people from where I'm from don't even get the chance to imagine. I've worked hard. I've kept moving. I've ticked the boxes.

But maybe I've been chasing more than just survival. Maybe I've been trying to live a life that isn't just successful, but *noble*. Not just hard-won, but *honorable*.

And yet, even now, I'm not always sure what any of it has meant. *What exactly have I been trying to prove? And who am I trying to prove it to?*

For most of my adult life, I've moved through the world with a constant sense of urgency. I've rarely slept more than three or four hours a night. I juggle roles — lawyer, nurse, business owner, writer — not only because I'm ambitious, but because stopping has always felt dangerous.

For years, I told myself I only had one life, so I needed to make the most of it. But lately I've begun to wonder if I confused that with a fear of slowing down. *If I ever stopped moving, would everything I'd built fall apart?*

So, I built a life of constant motion. Every time I settled into a role, I began scanning for the next one. Another degree. Another exam. Another reinvention.

Stillness and I have never been on good terms. Every time I try to rest, my brain tells me. *Cute. Now get up and apply for another license.* I wasn't unhappy. I just didn't know how to be still.

No one gave me a blueprint for what stillness looked like. In fact, it felt like forgetting to refresh a webpage — unnatural, inefficient, faintly threatening.

In my world, motion meant survival. You stop, you fall behind. Or worse, you disappear. So, you learn to move quickly, stay alert, and armor up for whatever the moment demands.

And yet in rare pauses, on long flights, after hard shifts, late at night, I'd find myself jotting things down. Notes on my phone. Scraps in MS Word docs. Fragments of thoughts on Notion I didn't yet know how to name.

Looking back, I see they were trying to tell me *something*.

—

As a nurse, I learned how to stay steady in chaos. How to care for people without needing thanks. How to make fast decisions that sometimes meant life or death.

As a lawyer, I learned a different kind of endurance. How to speak with precision, how to keep emotion at bay, how to demonstrate competence like it was a second language.

Both careers asked everything of me. But neither asked me who I was beneath the layers of usefulness. In both worlds, I had to prove myself not just to others, but to myself.

Even in entrepreneurship and writing, that pattern continued. I walked into rooms where the rules were never written down. Where success depended on whether someone had already decided you belonged.

So, I overcompensated. I collected qualifications like armor — degrees, licenses, and *unprocessed trauma* — in alphabetical order, of course. Some people collect stamps. I collected proof.

I watched people with half my experience be assumed competent, while I had to prove mine twice, in a softer voice, with perfect grammar and a palatable backstory. It wasn't just tiring. It was *infuriating* to have the rules written by people who'd never had to read them or live by them. And yet, I tried to meet them anyway.

Not because I believed in the rules, but because I believed I could outlast them.

I kept going because there was no safety net. Just grit. Just the instinct to move forward. Or risk being erased. Some days I'm surprised I've made it this far. Other days, I'm simply tired of how hard it's been to stay here.

People get impressed. But they rarely know what they're impressed by. They don't see the pride I've swallowed just to smile through days that nearly broke me. They don't see the grit it took just to show up again and again. They don't see the night I came home from a 12-hour shift, still trembling with exhaustion, only to open my laptop and force my brain into business mode. Drafting plans, chasing funding, willing a miracle that might buy me a few hours of sleep before the next shift. They don't see the bar exam flashcards shoved between clinical notes. The legal textbooks tucked into hospital lockers. The hundreds of pages memorized on train rides, during breaks, in borrowed time that never felt like mine.

To some, I'm an algorithm glitch — too good to be believable. Suspicious, simply for existing. There aren't many of them, but their words cut deeper than even self-awareness can shield against. They leave wounds that whisper,
No matter what you do, you'll never belong here.

Some may not understand, or refuse to, but I know exactly how much this cost. The long days. The longer nights. The toll of being competent and questioned.

Still, it wears on you. Having to prove yourself many times over, and still not be enough. It erodes something in you. Even with all I've achieved, there have been moments I've felt like a fraud. Not because I've done something wrong, but because the gap between where I'm from and where I've ended up can still feel disorienting.

In some rooms, I feel like I've outgrown my beginnings. In others, like I snuck in through the side door and must explain how I got past security.

Eventually, I noticed a pattern. A thread I hadn't meant to write but couldn't help tracing. It lived in the margins. In the scraps. In the parts I kept trying to edit out.

There was a story here. A ledger of what I'd been carrying.

These weren't polished reflections or neat conclusions. They were persistent traces of what it meant to build a life in real time. While doubting. While trying. While grieving. And still, while continuing.

That's when it hit me. I wasn't just collecting credentials. I was collecting questions. About survival. About worth. About who I've had to become.

I didn't write this memoir because I had the answers. I wrote it because I finally slowed down long enough to hear the questions I'd been avoiding.

This memoir isn't tidy. No clean arc. No perfect transformation. This is a record of what stayed standing. I don't write from wounds that haven't healed. I write from the scar tissue: the parts that held, even when it hurt.

Some of these stories are personal. Others, professional. Some trace grief. Others, joy. But all of them trace the same path — the journey of life — messy, complicated, but mine.

My noble and honorable adventure.

Maybe I wasn't just building a life. Maybe I was building wings. One exam, one shift, one risk at a time. And maybe they were never meant to carry me away. Just remind me I already knew how to rise.

So now I set down the armor. To believe I belong. Not because I proved it, but because I do. To touch the soil I came from. Not to prove I've made it, but to remember who I was before I had to. Before the titles. Before the miles. Before I learned that my roots weren't just anchors; they were wings, too.

Maybe the bravest thing I'll ever do is stop chasing the arc —

And *begin.*

PART I:
IDENTITY

Chapter 1: Roots Before Wings

Identity is a strange thing. It's both the roots that hold you in place and the wings that carry you forward. It's shaped by where you come from, the people who raised you, and the land that held your first steps.

For me, those roots are deep in Gubatan, a place where time moves at its own pace, where the smell of earth and the sound of roosters are as familiar as my own name.

Gubatan is not the kind of place that shows up on glossy postcards. Unless your idea of paradise includes goats mid-strut, clotheslines swaying like dancers caught in a breeze, and your neighbor's banana trees basking in the late afternoon light like reluctant influencers.

Tucked in the foothills of Mount Apo, in a peaceful corner of the municipality of Magpet, Cotabato, in the Philippines, Gubatan is a *barangay* of dirt roads, rusted roofs, and chickens that cross not just streets but entire yards with the audacity of elected officials. The air often carries the scent of woodsmoke and ripening jackfruit, and whatever the weather feels like whispering that day.

When it rains, as it often does, the earth doesn't just drink. It gulps. You can hear it. The gentle hiss of droplets on banana leaves, the soft patter on tin roofs, the muddy gurgle of water carving paths down foot-worn trails. The soil releases a scent both ancient and intimate. A warm, loamy perfume that clings to your slippers, to your soul, and, if you're lucky, to your memory.

Gubatan, like the rest of Magpet, is green. Wildly, insistently green. Neither manicured nor curated. The kind of green that grows back no matter how many times you hack it down. The kind that reminds you nature has the final say.

At first, my roots felt like burdens — heavy with expectations, slowed by tradition, and tethered to a pace that felt at odds with my dreams. I thought I had to break free to move forward.

But with time, I saw that those roots were never chains. They were the foundation. The bedrock from which my strength grew. They gave me resilience to endure, wisdom to navigate a world far beyond Gubatan, and the courage to spread my wings and soar.

I was born here in 1986 — November 22, to be exact. At home. No hospital gowns. No epidurals. Just *Manang* Perla, the *barangay* midwife, my mother's grit, and Halley's Comet somewhere in the sky, probably wondering what it had landed me into.

To me, Gubatan wasn't *'rural'* or *'remote.'* It wasn't a category. It was just life. It was normal to wake up to roosters with scheduling issues, to eat boiled rice with whatever was available — sometimes *pan de sal*, mostly dried fish, or *bulad*, as we'd call it — and to live in a wooden house on stilts, where the walls didn't just breathe, but listened. The wind came through bamboo slats, carrying voices. Prayers, arguments, gossip, and the occasional karaoke betrayal.

Everyone knew your name, your family tree, your crush, and whether you had passed your exams. You could lie to your parents, but not to your neighbors. Gubatan was the original Facebook, but without the algorithm and with more chickens.

I was the youngest of eight, which meant I inherited everything. Clothes, chores, and a nickname, *Nonoy*, which I'm still trying to outgrow. Our house stood just across from Sibug Elementary School, where my mother taught and I studied. My classroom was visible from our kitchen window. Some kids cried on their first day of school. I just grabbed my bag and crossed the street like I was picking up *kamote*.

Our mother — *Nanay* — calm, composed, with a side-eye sharp enough to slice cassava, or *balanghoy* in Cebuano dialect, once silenced an entire classroom with just a glance, and could correct your grammar mid-sentence while ladling *law-oy* into your bowl.

Her discipline wasn't loud; it was surgical. Her humor? Dry as overcooked tilapia, but just as unforgettable. She was the kind of woman who could make you question your life choices with a single eyebrow, and then feed you right after, because discipline and love came served on the same plate, taught with chalk dust on her skirt and compassion in her voice.

Our father — *Tatay* — a farmer with a face carved by the sun and a will harder than the soil he tilled, was perpetually feared. He woke us early every weekend with the same declaration, *"Bring your slippers. We leave in five."* It wasn't a request; it was ritual. We weeded, planted, and harvested beneath a sun that never negotiated, our backs bent in silent obedience to seasons we didn't control. The air smelled of crushed grass, overripe fruit, and sweat-soaked earth.

We grew crops as bold as our family spirit: *rambutan* with their mischievous hairs and fiery red skins, *durian* with their spiked defiance, *marang* with their sticky sweetness, and mandarin trees that whispered orange promises with every breeze.

Transporting them was another adventure. The crates, two on each side, were balanced on the back of Babes, our grumpy but loyal horse. Either my sister Giegie, boyish and brave, or my brother Toto, hardened at a young age by the weight of Tatay's demands and expectations, led the charge down the steep hills of Pangao-an, a *barangay* nestled deeper in the hills than our own Gubatan. They'd whistle commands as Babes clopped over rocks and roots, the load swaying like a slow, earthy parade of rural resilience. The journey from the farm to the Poblacion wasn't just a delivery, it was our version of economy. A slow, earthy declaration of grit and resilience.

Tatay never said *"I love you."* His love was measured in labor. In the sweat-stained shirts and the calluses that spoke louder than any words. His love was in the early mornings, when we rose before the sun, so we would never go to bed hungry.

We had a television that worked when the weather felt generous. Otherwise, we needed to maneuver the pole antenna to try to get a better signal. If that didn't work, we gathered at the neighbor's house to watch the news, or *teleseryes* — those long-running Filipino soap operas (*Mara Clara, Esperanza*) — where no one ever changed clothes but somehow always changed hearts. There was no such thing as binge-watching. There was waiting. And somehow, the waiting made it better.

Entertainment was communal, just like the way we lived. We had less, but we laughed more. Life was simple. We were poor in cash, but rich in chaos, story, and meaning.

At school, even at a young age, I already sensed that I was different. While the other boys played basketball and roughhoused in the dust, I wrote screenplays in my head and rehearsed monologues to the trees. My classmates talked about crushes; I talked about characters. I didn't have the language for it then — only a sense of being elsewhere, even when I was present. An ache that I carried like a second skin.

At the time, being different felt like a flaw. Now I see it for what it was: a *foreshadowing*. A hidden strength.

Books were my escape hatch. I'd lie under mango trees, borrowing textbooks meant for older students, reading about places I couldn't pronounce and lives I couldn't afford, but imagined myself stepping into anyway. Back then, I didn't see it as escape. I saw it as practice. A rehearsal for a life that felt both impossible and inevitable. I didn't know where, but I knew I was going. Somewhere far. Somewhere true.

That early hunger to understand a bigger world planted the seeds of every leap I would take later. Across professions, across countries, across my own limits. That was the beginning, even if I didn't yet have the words for it.

And while not Instagrammable, fairy-tale perfect, I had a happy childhood. Solid. Warm. Tender in its own rough way. We had drama — sure. But we also had love. Not the movie kind. The rural kind. One that shows up in corrected grammar, in saved portions of food, in knowing someone will always be on your side even when they're scolding you.

By the time I graduated from Magpet National High School in 2002, the soil of Gubatan had already done its work on me. Firming my steps, sharpening my instincts, and embedding in me a sense that every test, academic or otherwise, was just another version of walking barefoot through our family's farm — unpredictable, humbling, and full of small lessons waiting in the dirt.

I understood two things. First, education would be my only passport. Second, kindness — not cleverness — would be my true currency. These lessons, planted deep, would take years to bloom. But bloom they did.

This is not a rags-to-riches story. This is a *roots-before-wings* story. A hymn to the soil that raised me, not the spotlight that found me. If there's any arc here, it's not about escape. It's about return. To self. To truth. To the green that refuses to be forgotten.

The further I moved from Gubatan, the clearer it became. I didn't need to escape my roots. I needed to embrace them. And once I did, life stopped feeling like an accident. And started feeling like flight.

My wings didn't grow in spite of my roots; they grew because of them.
Wide enough to carry me across oceans, brave enough to chase ideas beyond what was expected, and strong enough to lead me to a life of noble and honorable adventures, to places I once thought only existed in books. From Manila to Wellington, the Gold Coast to Brisbane, Paris to Frankfurt, New York to Sydney. And even further afield.

And now, with every step forward, I carry those roots with me — not as weight, but as compass.

Soul Notes

❖ What values shaped you long before you had the words for them, before résumés, roles, or cities ever tried to define you?

❖ What if your past wasn't a weight to overcome, but a foundation holding you upright?

❖ And if you peeled back the layers — the titles, timelines, and expectations — what part of you still feels like home?

Chapter 2: Sticky Lessons: Leadership and Lollies

Gubatan had grounded me in grit. High school would stretch it into something more. Leadership shaped by the everyday work of showing up. My roots had held me firm. Now, they'd be tested in the heat, hustle, and hormonal chaos of Magpet National High School.

Leadership and lollies may sound light, or unrelated. But together, they taught me how to balance responsibility with joy. To step up, and still savor the small, sticky things.

In high school, I didn't just discover public speaking or student leadership. I discovered *yema*. Filipino sticky, sweet candies of condensed milk and egg yolk stirred over low flame until it thickened. And with it, the earliest lessons in entrepreneurship, influence, and trust.

The days at school stretched just enough to let the drama in. Every recess break pulsed with the promise of a new teenage saga. Heat was a constant companion, clinging to our uniforms like wet laundry, mixing with the sharp scent of disinfectant and crushed guava leaves from the campus hedges. The cracked concrete hallways echoed with a daily symphony, shrieking whistles from the P.E. field, the scrape of monobloc chairs on tiled floors, and the rhythmic clapping of teachers signalling silence that was almost always ignored.

Hormones surged like monsoon rivers — overwhelming, unpredictable, and capable of flooding entire classrooms with drama in under ten seconds. Acne bloomed across foreheads and cheeks like little rebellions. Hair gel gleamed under the sun like armor. Deodorants battled valiantly but often lost by midday. In this humid pressure cooker of adolescence, everything felt urgent. Friendships, grades, crushes, dreams.

The library, a once-peaceful sanctuary, had transformed into a battleground. Under buzzing fluorescent lights and the occasional flicker from a dying bulb, the low hum of electric fans barely masking whispered gossip, the rustle of notebook pages doubling as cover for flirtatious notes passed under tables. There, academic rivalry simmered beside stolen glances. Eyes meeting briefly over the tops of textbooks, hearts pounding harder than any quiz result could justify.

Our classrooms smelled of chalk, floor wax, and adolescent ambition. The kind that clung to you like sweat and hope. It was in these sun-drenched, overcrowded rooms that I first began to feel the subtle pulse of purpose. Each creak of the blackboard, each faint smudge of white dust on our uniforms felt like an initiation. Into curiosity, into courage, into the power of having something to say. It was here that I discovered the power of words. I joined speech contests, writing competitions, and student government (because clearly, I wasn't busy enough).

I wasn't loud, but I was listened to. And that made all the difference. Teachers noticed. Classmates asked me for help on essays. Something in me ignited. That words, when used well, could move hearts, impress crushes, and shake systems.

But I wasn't alone in that hunger. There were others — Dennis, Randy, Jieger, Milay — classmates who rose like cream to the top of every class, fueled by sheer grit. They came from families like mine, where *baon* was a prayer and notebooks were recycled. We understood, even then, that there were no shortcuts. Only sweat, persistence, and faith. We weren't competing with each other. We were outrunning limitation together.

And then there was Rodel. Blind, but never behind. Every day, he arrived with his braille notes, his calm dignity, and a determination fiercer than any of ours. We weren't a special education class. Just a typical, underfunded public school. But Rodel kept up anyway and refused to be left behind. Or tried. And in trying, he taught us more than any teacher ever did. He was one of my earliest quiet giants. It was through him I learned that difference has many forms — some visible, some not — and some, like his, come with a name and a lesson in courage.

Leadership, I discovered, wasn't in the title. It was in those early, unnoticed acts — the small kindnesses, the unannounced battles, the invisible labors.

Later in life, when I'd wear suits instead of uniforms and lead teams instead of stacking chairs, I would still draw from these moments. These early tests of character became my blueprint for leadership — humble, observant, and grounded in service rather than show.

It was in the unglamorous details. Sweeping the classroom after everyone had left, or offering your umbrella to someone who forgot theirs in the rain. It was remembering who had a sick grandmother, who needed help with math, who always came to school hungry.

Outside school, life was still a mix of responsibilities. Farm chores, family duties, and the occasional community dance number. After school, I'd return to the heat of our kitchen, where the scent of rice and boiled eggs greeted me before I could kick off my shoes. Then came the *yema* operation. I'd let it cool just enough to wrap in makeshift cellophane pieces, some with reused candy logos still faintly visible. My fingertips would be dusted with sugar, my bag with small ambitions wrapped in cellophane.

Each piece sold was a small win. Not just in pesos but in proof. That effort mattered. That my hands could turn hope into something sweet and trade it for belief. It taught me more than math ever could about self-worth, resilience, the courage of showing up with hope in a paper bag, and how sometimes, even unpaid candies are lessons in trust and the art of letting go. Until a classmate would flash a sheepish grin and snatch two without paying. *"Bayaran taka ugma, promise,"* (*"I will pay you tomorrow, I promise"*) they'd say, voice syrupy with charm. I was learning, painfully, that entrepreneurship required optimism and a high tolerance for IOUs.

High school taught me that leadership isn't always about speeches, medals, or some grand ambition, but a series of small, sticky lessons — *yema* beside math books, IOUs in schoolbags, kindness passed hand to hand.

Those sticky *yema* afternoons, as trivial as they seemed, were the first pages of my financial education. Long before I opened a bank account or learned what a spreadsheet was, I was already doing the math: costing ingredients, estimating margins, negotiating IOUs, and learning — sometimes the hard way — that not all debts are repaid in pesos. They weren't just sweets; they were business prototypes. Rehearsals for the acumen I'd later need to run a law firm, build systems, manage cash flow, and price value without undervaluing myself.

And it makes you think — *Why don't we teach more of that in school?* We spend years drilling trigonometry and memorising historical dates, but we leave budgeting, negotiation, and real-world resilience for life to teach. Often after it's already too expensive to fail.

I'm grateful for the academics. But I wish someone had told us that selling *yema* was economics. That handling money, even in coins, was financial literacy. That wrapping candy and managing classmates' IOUs was business strategy in disguise. Schools may focus on textbooks, but some of the most important subjects are still being taught, unofficially, on the margins of the curriculum.

As high school was nearing its end, something had shifted. I wasn't just dreaming anymore. I was planning. Plotting. Planting seeds in the dark and trusting they would bloom. I had my eyes set on San Pedro College in Davao City, one of Mindanao's top nursing schools. A goal that once felt too far, now suddenly within reach.

My parents raised eight children on little more than cassava, courage, and calendar prayers. Those tiny tear-off sheets marked with saints and suppers we couldn't always afford. And my sister Febbie? She left for Saudi Arabia to work, so I could go to school.

My family believed in me. That kind of belief — steady, sacrificial, stubborn — was the push. The steady drumbeat behind every bold move I'd make. It hummed beneath everything, like a secret anthem I never stopped hearing.

Carrying early lessons in leadership and economics, I'd pack my *yema*-stained notebooks and board a Weena bus to Davao City. A duffel bag of borrowed dreams in one hand, and the lessons of Magpet stitched into my spine. San Pedro College would test everything I thought I knew about ambition, identity, and what it means to care. But for now, I was still just a kid with candy in his bag and fire in his belly. Already leading, already learning.

Soul Notes

❖ When did responsibility shape you before you noticed it?

❖ What invisible acts taught you how to lead?

❖ What sweetness from your past still lingers, not on your tongue, but in your memory?

Chapter 3: Empathy with Edge

I entered college not as a blank slate, but as a man already tempered by *yema*, floor wax, and the grind of leadership. High school taught me how to care privately. Nursing school would now teach me how to do it publicly. In institutions, on paper, and often in spite of how I felt.

Empathy may be soft, but it's often forged under fluorescent lights and bureaucratic madness. Sometimes, it looks like staying up all night to memorize diseases you don't care about. Because someone told you this is your future. When sharpened by resistance, empathy becomes something else: an *edge*. A kind of knowing. A way of seeing the world not just with compassion, but with conviction.

They say college is where you *'find yourself.'* I always found that phrase suspicious. As if the self were a sock that slipped behind a dorm fridge and just needed rescuing. I believe that identity is forged. Often painfully. Through sleepless nights, cafeteria meals of questionable origin, and the long, aching stretch of silence where no one is clapping, but you show up anyway.

I arrived in Davao City, a city roughly 2 hours away from Gubatan (4 hours under heavy traffic) with hand-me-down dreams and laundry soap that still smelled like our backyard. The city shimmered with tricycle horns, jeepney barkers, diesel fumes, and the sticky smell of *durian* and vinegar. It was hot in a way that made your back sweat just by blinking. And yet, beneath the chaos, Davao had rhythm. And I, somehow, found mine.

San Pedro College was a cathedral of quiet panic. It had a reputation for two things: academic excellence, and making students cry by midterms. The corridors smelled like antiseptic, photocopy ink, and unresolved trauma. The whiteboards never fully erased, so ghostly anatomy sketches lingered like half-formed regrets.

Nursing wasn't my first choice. Law was. I dreamed of courtrooms, not clinics. Latin phrases, not IV flushes. I wanted black robes, not white uniforms. Back then, I would've said, *"I wanted to serve the Filipino people."* And I meant it — I still do. Only now, I understand that service wears many uniforms.

In the Philippines, dreams often require committee approval. Auntie Belen's immigration success, a neighbor's daughter thriving in Hong Kong, the relentless myth that America solves everything. They all weighed in. Nursing was practical. Nursing was portable. Law was noble, but indulgent. So, I chose the dream that promised migration. Or perhaps, it chose me.

Simone de Beauvoir once wrote, *"One is not born, but rather becomes."* And no one dreams of shift rotations or memorizing drug contraindications. At least not me. We simply learn to survive them. With precision, patience, and the stubborn hope that they might lead somewhere worth going.

At first, I resisted. Nursing felt like duty dressed in white. But it had gravity. And soon, it began to shape me. I did what scholarship kids like me would do. I adapted. Studied harder. Laughed through the stress. Learned to calculate IV drip rates while holding onto a future that didn't yet feel like mine. I wasn't in love with nursing, but I was beginning to respect what it demanded of me.

During nursing lectures, the air in our classrooms was a cocktail of ambition, sweat, and Milo powder. Nights were filled with whispered prayers and highlighters scratching through a thousand pages of Tortora's Anatomy and Physiology textbook. We moved like ghosts. Bleary-eyed, caffeine-fueled, but stubborn.

And then came the hospital. Everything we memorized in class got real, fast. No more case studies, no more multiple choice. Just people, pain, and the pressure to show up like you knew what you were doing, even when your hands were shaking. Once, I held a stranger's wrist — neither in friendship nor flirtation — but to feel the pulse that told me whether they were still alive. It was my first hospital shift as a student nurse, and within minutes, it was already a *Code Brown* (brown matter was involved). I remember thinking: *What did I get myself into?*

This wasn't the kind of heroism nursing posters had promised. But after the chaos, the clean-up, the caregiving, the patient looked at me, held my hand, and whispered thank you with a sincerity that cracked something open in me. A humane moment that made me understand what true empathy felt like — messy, humbling, and oddly sacred.

Still, nursing education wasn't easy. That empathy was tested by pressure, by people, and by a system that confused fear for excellence. In second year, something strange happened. A professor pursuing his PhD decided to turn our class into a live research experiment. The smartest students in the year, myself included, were plucked and grouped into a single section. We became the statistical variable, the experimental group; another section as the control. Both guinea pigs. Consent wasn't exactly a hot topic then. We didn't question it much. I belonged in a generation that just adjusted our uniforms and got on with it. But looking back, that *'elite'* group felt more like a pressure cooker than a privilege.

That year tested us. We were supposed to be the best, but what that meant was being scrutinized more, pressured harder, expected to perform without breaking. The honor felt hollow. The excellence came with exhaustion. And beneath the lab coats and textbooks, truth began to surface. That real care can't grow in fear.

The culture of nursing instruction? Let's just say, at least in my experience, it confused compassion with cruelty. Respect was often conflated with fear. Kindness was optional. Excellence meant endurance. Some clinical instructors seemed to believe that humiliation built resilience — and maybe it did, but not without collateral damage.

During one clinical demo, I had a full-on nursing brain freeze. My hands shook, my IV tubing tangled like Christmas lights, and for a second, I genuinely forgot which end of the stethoscope went where. My instructor gave feedback with the gentleness of a military boot camp. Loud, surgical, and witnessed by everyone. I chuckled along like it was no big deal, but five minutes later, I was in an empty hall questioning all my life choices while trying not to cry on my white uniform.

We were studying to become healers, yet sometimes, the system wounded us first.

But then, Ma'am Sarah saw me crying in the corner, trying (and failing) to look like I was just interested in the tiles. She didn't offer some grand speech or motivational quote. She just sat beside me, no words said, like someone who cared more about people than protocol. We didn't say much. We didn't need to. Her presence said enough. Years later, she would become the dean of the College of Nursing — and in that moment, I knew the school was in good hands.

That rigidity created something formidable. Filipino nurses are among the best in the world. We export care the way others export coffee or copper. In many households, it's not just a profession, it's the family business model and economic backbone. We're trained to serve, but rarely celebrated. Respected abroad, underpaid at home. Entitlement never made it into our textbooks. Endurance did.

I just wish we didn't have to be broken to be brilliant. That excellence didn't require trauma. That rigor didn't have to look like fear. But then again, some fires do forge diamonds. I'm just not sure we all had to burn that long to shine.

Throughout those four years of nursing studies, I kept trying to find avenues to tolerate nursing. Hence, I joined the SPC Debating Club. That's where I first learned that ideas could be both weapons and shields. That logic, when paired with a little humor and a raised eyebrow, could win over even the most biased judges. It was there I learned how to speak. To argue truth into the room.

I still remember one debate competition where my team had to argue in favor of legalizing divorce, a stance that at the time clashed with everything my upbringing taught me. I almost backed out. But as I stood at the podium, voice trembling but steady, something shifted. I wasn't just delivering arguments; I was confronting belief, articulating truths I hadn't fully admitted to myself. By the time I finished, the judges were silent, then nodding.

We won. But more than that, I did. I walked off that stage breathless, not from fear, but from fire. I felt alive in a way nursing never gave me — sharp, electric, sure. Debate didn't just awaken my voice. It awakened a part of me that had been waiting backstage for a mic.

And then, I found The Rock. The student publication. Wedged in a forgotten hallway and always short on toner, it became my second home. I joined as a staff writer. Later, Editor-in-Chief. While classmates memorized SOAP notes, I wrote editorials on poverty, politics, and the Filipino diaspora. That's also where Joan, my best friend, and I collided. Joan was also from the province. Practical, sharp, unshakable. Nursing wasn't her passion either, but she excelled anyway. Later, she too would become a lawyer. In our final year of nursing studies, she led the student council, Saligan, while I ran The Rock. We were often at odds, as it is often natural for the press to criticize politicians — not out of ego, but intensity. Battle of the brains. A clash of two people who cared and argued like they were born for a courtroom. But it was never personal. We sharpened each other. Sometimes with sarcasm, sometimes with silence. We were proof that iron sharpens iron.

Between The Rock and the SPC Debating Club, I began to feel the stirrings of something larger than the degree I was finishing. At the time, I didn't fully grasp it. But now I know. Those were my origin stories.

Nursing taught me how to care. Journalism taught me how to question. Debating taught me how to advocate. Together, they gave me a strange alchemy: *empathy with edge.*

They were laying the blueprint for the life I live now. Equal parts stethoscope and statute, care and conviction, service and speech. Nursing and law. Who knew?

Still, life was lived in extremes. One day I'd be leading a community vaccination program in a remote *barangay*. The next, I'd be editing a piece about overseas Filipino workers and the ethics of economic migration. My days began at 5 a.m. and ended with my face in a textbook. My hands smelled like Betadine; my heart, of hunger. My brain couldn't decide if it belonged in a ward or a newsroom. And yet, I kept going. Because I already believed then that I wasn't built for mediocrity. But for meaning. And, apparently, multitasking with flair.

In 2006, I graduated cum laude. The applause was loud, but what I remember most is turning to Nanay and asking her to buy me a new Nokia phone. She hesitated. We did not have the capacity, and I knew that, but pride has a way of making you bold, sometimes foolish. She said yes out of love. Looking back, I wish I hadn't asked. That phone is long gone. But the cost of that sacrifice stays with me. One of my earliest regrets, wrapped in a moment of pride.

That same year, I dipped my toes into the glamorous world of call centers. By day, I was a nurse-in-training reviewing for the Philippine Nurse Licensure Exam; by night, I was a voice in a headset, diffusing the rage of middle America over dropped signals and defective remotes. It sounds chaotic, but I loved the duality. There was something exhilarating about switching lives in the span of a bus ride. One world taught me clinical precision. The other demanded corporate polish. One was about healing the body. The other, calming tempers over broadband outages.

At that call center in the IT Park in Cebu, I wore a headset, memorized the phonetic alphabet, and learned to pronounce '*Illinois*' properly while getting yelled at by Americans about their cable bills. The fluorescent lights were brutal. The midnight shift was soul-sucking. But it taught me patience, composure, and how to manage pressure with a smile in my voice. It was a strange rehearsal for adulthood. One where code-switching was currency and duality, survival. I was living two lives. And somehow, both were real.

We were paid just enough to survive, not enough to indulge. Jollibee, the beacon of middle-class joy, was too expensive most days. I'd watch people order Chicken Joy like they were royalty. Meanwhile, I stuck to instant noodles and whatever canned goods were on sale. On lucky nights, when overtime paid out or the existential dread of another shift felt too heavy, I'd treat myself to The Coffee Bean or Starbucks. But most days, it was *ngo hiong*, rice, and cold Coke in a plastic cup, but that even felt like luxury. We sat under flickering lights, talked about call metrics and quarter-life crises, and pretended this was just a pit stop to something better. And maybe, deep down, we knew it was.

My call center contract finished in time to allow me exactly 7 days to fully review the exam material. It was hectic. After passing the exam (first try, thank you very much), I headed to St. Luke's Medical Center in Quezon City. The uniforms were tighter, the stakes higher. But even there, the pen never left me. It lived in the margins of shift reports and whispered itself into patient notes.

The nurse in me charted vitals. The writer in me charted the soul.

I didn't know it then, but my choices laid the foundation for a life that would demand both precision and poetry. Nursing studies and The Rock/SPC Debating Club. Nursing review and call center. A life where the scalpel and the sentence, the wound and the word, would learn to coexist.

We aren't born whole. We grow into ourselves. Piece by piece, stumble by stumble. And if we're lucky — if we listen to our hunger and honor our detours — we don't just become what we're told, we become ourselves.

—

In Davao and in Cebu, I built myself. Out of mismatched dreams and midnight study sessions, call center shifts and campus crusades. There, I learned to care without being crushed. To question without being cruel. To argue with purpose and listen with sincerity.

That's what empathy with edge looks like. A heart that cuts and cares in equal measure. And maybe that's the point.

Identity isn't about choosing between being soft or strong — it's about becoming both.

In the end I didn't find myself settling in either city. Davao and Cebu were only the first training grounds where empathy grew edges and edges learned wisdom. What waited in Manila would be louder, meaner, messier. A new arena where my voice would be tested, my compassion stretched, and my convictions dragged into the ring. I didn't know it yet, but everything this chapter gave me — the pen, the mic, the edge — I'd soon need to wield them all.

This chapter of my life was the apprenticeship of empathy, sharp enough to cut through anything that came next.

—

Gubatan gave me roots. Davao sparked ambition. And nursing taught me how to listen. Not just with stethoscopes, but with presence. These early chapters shaped my sense of self in often unspoken ways.

Identity, I came to realize, isn't something you inherit fully formed. It's something you grow into, question, carry, and sometimes rewrite. But knowing who you are is only the beginning. The real test is what you do with that knowledge — how you move through the world when comfort fades and conviction is all you have left.

That's where *courage* begins.

Soul Notes

❖ When did you first realize you weren't just one thing and that you could lead, serve, dream, and still be learning?

❖ What unexpected strength or insight came from a role you didn't choose, but carried anyway?

❖ How do you honor the version of you that showed up while making space for the one still becoming?

PART II: COURAGE

Chapter 4: SkyFlakes, Sacrifice, and Survival

Courage doesn't always look like defiance. Sometimes, it's SkyFlakes for dinner. A Filipino cracker tucked into purses and pantries like a survival kit, a four-hour commute, and a silent prayer that you don't mess up a medication chart.

It begins not with heroics, but hesitation. A trembling yes to a job you're not ready for, but there is willingness to walk into fear anyway.

This part of the story isn't about grandeur. It's about grit.

There's no preparing for your first real hospital job (not even while still high on the fumes of my cum laude certificate). Especially not in Metro Manila, where the heat feels personal, like it's trying to crawl under your skin. The streets hum with tension. Jeepneys sputter and jostle for space, their sides painted with religious decals and stickers peeling from years of sun. Sidewalks smell of fishballs, gasoline, and the slow burn of a city constantly on edge.

The traffic in the metro moves like grief. Slow, stubborn, and indifferent to your urgency. It doesn't just delay you; it taunts you. Engines idling in concert, jeepneys coughing up black smoke, vendors weaving through lanes selling boiled peanuts and hope.

Metro Manila is a living, groaning beast — honking, grinding, sweating — and somehow you have to arrive at work looking semi-professional, not like you wrestled your way out of a sauna on wheels.

In Gubatan, I carried water jugs uphill. In Manila, I carried heavy, sacred, often unspeakable stories. Different loads, same spine.

By the time I arrived at St. Luke's Medical Center in Quezon City in 2007, I was already sweating through my white uniform. The air inside was sterile and cold, a jarring contrast to the chaos outside. The polished floors reflected harsh fluorescent lights, and the walls gleamed with a kind of clinical indifference. My shoes squeaked nervously with every step. My ID hung around my neck like both a badge and a burden. And as I inhaled the scent of antiseptic and freshly brewed panic, I realized this was no simulation; this was the real thing.

I was assigned to the Digestive and Liver Unit, a ward that smelled of alcohol swabs, overripe bananas, and anxiety. Monitors beeped in a discordant rhythm that never let you forget you were in a place that danced with life and death.

There was a man in the room at the unit's furthest end, late 60s, liver cancer, a voice like gravel wrapped in gratitude. Every morning, I'd find him praying over a photograph of his grandchildren. He never asked for much, just that his coffee be warm and his sheets be straight. One day, as I tucked the blanket under his feet, he said: *"You remind me of my son. If he were still alive, I'd want him to be like you."*

I swallowed hard, blinked back something sharp, and nodded. I didn't say much. But I came back the next day. And the day after that.

At the DLU, patients arrived pale, panicked, or already resigned. Some looked like they had fought too long; others hadn't yet begun. Amidst the chaos, it was dazzling. The machines beeped in three languages. The nurses operated like clockwork with coffee addictions. Patients came in with VIP insurance cards and attitudes to match. And here I was, a small-town lad from Gubatan, trying not to drop the bedpan.

My hands trembled the first time I had to change a colostomy bag. I flushed the first time I mispronounced a medication in front of a consultant. I learned quickly. Manila doctors walk fast, talk faster, and expect you to follow without stumbling. There was no room for second guesses. Just quick glances, sharper notes, and a smile that said *"Yes, Doc"* even when your spine screamed otherwise.

On many occasions, I felt like a liability in scrubs while fumbling through routines, forgetting who was *nothing per orem* or NPO, and confusing tramadol with something that sounded like it but wasn't.

I was learning the work while wondering who I might become if I survived it. This wasn't just about learning how to hold a bedpan. It was about learning how to hold fear without flinching. To sit with doubt and still act. To walk into rooms full of pain and fluorescent judgment and choose not to disappear.

Somewhere along the way, beneath the antiseptic smell and the consultant's clipped instructions, something shifted. Maybe it was the way Nurse JR gave me a nod after I held a patient's hand through a painful procedure. Maybe it was the way the patient whispered *salamat* with cracked lips, reminding me that presence is what people remember. I started to understand: *Confidence doesn't come before competence.* It sneaks in gently, after you survive a dozen small humiliations — and still return.

DLU became my proving ground. I watched as families clung to one another in waiting rooms that never stopped buzzing. I witnessed recoveries that felt like miracles and losses that hung in the air like burnt toast — acrid, clinging, hard to ignore. The hardest moments weren't the loud ones; they were the ones that came in silence. A monitor flatlining, a family member's sob behind a curtain, the solemn nod of a doctor confirming what no one wanted to hear.

What began as a blur slowly hardened into something clearer. I found comfort in the repetition. Rolling IV stands down antiseptic hallways, flipping through charts that smelled faintly of ink and panic, offering a smile to patients too weak to return it. There was unspoken intimacy in wiping someone's fevered brow, in cleaning soiled private parts without judgment, in holding a hand just tightly enough to say, *"I see you."*

We found joy where we could. In nurses' pantries with lukewarm coffee. In midnight *harutan* between vitals checks. In *pansit*, the unofficial currency of gratitude. We loved it, don't get me wrong. But every nurse knew the rule. When a patient brings a platter of it to the nurses' station, brace yourself, the shift is about to go to hell. Somehow, without fail, that foil tray of greasy noodles was the harbinger of chaos. We'd accept it with a smile, all while mentally preparing for three codes, a vomiting patient, and a missing chart. We called it the curse of celebratory carbs.

And in between the panic and the procedures, we laughed. Not because it was funny, but because it was the only way to stay whole. Nurses know how to laugh not because things are easy, but because they're not. We found humor in badly translated discharge instructions, in phantom calls from patients who just wanted company, in the daily absurdity of being human under pressure. Sometimes, we laughed just to stay upright.

As I was getting used to the hospital life, I thought courage would feel like confidence. But more often, I found it felt like doubt held in silence. Like coming back the next day. And the next.

Living in the metro taught me about independence. We did 8-hour shifts, which sounded reasonable until you realized you had to be there almost every day of the week. Combine that with 4-hour commutes to and from the house where I lived, and the culinary joys of canned tuna and SkyFlakes, you had a lifestyle powered by pure grit. This was 2008, after all. There was no Lazada, no GrabFood, and no TikTok to distract us. Just SMS promos and hoping the MRT wasn't packed like a can of sardines.

That life — Metro Manila 2008 — wasn't romantic. It was SkyFlakes, sacrifice, and survival. Dry crackers in my pocket, aching feet in second-hand shoes, and just enough hope to clock in again the next day. That's what kept me going. Not some grand ambition, but the subtle decision to endure. To serve. To grow.

It was overwhelming. It was exhausting. And somehow, it became one of the best times of my life.

Amidst the madness, I found rhythm. I found friendships. I found the kind of teamwork that isn't about titles but about trust. The unspoken bond between a nurse handing over a patient at shift change and another taking over like they've known them their whole life.

Mommy Liz, Ma'am Juvy, Ivy, Karen, Tine, Angie, Vic, Isa, etc — colleagues and later friends etched into a chapter of my life I'll never forget. But deep down, I knew I couldn't stay forever. I wanted to see what else was out there. Not just geographically, but personally.

There was an itch beneath the routine. Not for escape, exactly, but for expansion. For homes I hadn't yet named. For versions of myself I hadn't yet met.

Metro Manila didn't just teach me how to endure. It taught me how to listen. Beneath the honks, the cries, the clang of call bells. For the *whisper.*

The real shift wasn't just in geography. It was in me. Somewhere between the SkyFlakes and the silence, between the call bells and cracked lips whispering *salamat*, I stopped needing to prove I belonged and started becoming someone who did.

Courage hadn't arrived like I expected — with certainty or swelling music — but in the ordinary ritual of returning. And some faces stayed, like the man I looked after in the unit's furthest end, whose soft thanks still hums beneath every shift I've worked since.

Metro Manila invited me to show up scared, sweaty, and unsure, and to do it anyway. And every day that I did, I learned: *SkyFlakes may crumble. But I don't.*

That whisper would eventually take me to New Zealand. To a different kind of silence, a different kind of strength. And I listened. Not because I was certain, but because I was curious.

I wasn't running away from the chaos. I was carrying its lessons with me. SkyFlakes still in my bag. Calluses still on my feet. But now, I was headed toward skies I'd never seen, with just enough courage to begin *again*.

Soul Notes

❖ What experience forced you to grow stronger because you had to?

❖ When did you feel the first pull to stretch beyond who you thought you were or what others expected of you?

❖ What did surviving look like in a season when you had to perform but didn't feel prepared?

Chapter 5: Kia Ora

America was always the plan. Like many Filipino nurses, I had my eyes set on the United States of America. That mythical land of opportunity where the burger is bigger, the grass is greener, and remittance was both duty and redemption. I had my papers ready, my timeline drawn.

But then the 2008 Global Financial Crisis hit like a slammed door. U.S. hospitals froze hiring, visa retrogression swept through like a cold front, and suddenly, the promised land wasn't promising anything.

The path was blocked, but not gone. America would circle back into my story later, like a delayed flight (It will beckon again later in life). But for now, New Zealand was softly, persistently calling, like a door I hadn't meant to knock on, but was now slightly ajar.

New Zealand was never part of the plan. Then again, neither was nursing. But life, in its strange, sneaky brilliance, tends to shove you toward the right doors whether you were planning to knock or not.

It started with a job application and a sense of adventure. Also, let's be real, Manila traffic will drive anyone to consider immigration. The idea of fresh air, safer streets, and a work-life balance that didn't involve MRT survival mode was irresistible.

In 2011, I landed in Palmerston North, a town so still I could hear my thoughts echo back at me, as if the air itself had time to listen. After years of Manila's concrete chaos and the never-ending drone of tricycles and traffic, this sudden stillness was almost alien.

The sky felt stretched wider here, like it had finally nothing to prove. The wind carried the clean scent of damp grass and distant hay, and the silence was broken only by the occasional lowing of cows or the crisp crunch of leaves under your uncertain steps. Drivers stopped at pedestrian crossings. Some even waved you on with a smile, their windows rolled down, arms tanned and relaxed. The roads were orderly, so absurdly peaceful. Walking down them felt like stepping into a carefully rendered dream. No honking, no shouting, no chaos. Just the steady hum of a place that didn't need to hurry. I kept waiting for someone to yell *"Cut!"* like I was an extra in a simulation of peace.

After the initial *"Kia Ora!"* by the educational facility, I was taken to a tiny town on New Zealand's North Island west coast called Foxton for the Competence Assessment Programme, a 6-week bridging course required for overseas-trained nurses to prove competence in local healthcare standards. In the dead of winter, no less. It was bitterly cold, the kind that wraps around your bones and makes your breath visible like ghostly punctuation in the air. That's where I met Alynne, also from Davao, and instantly, we bonded. Both of us had borrowed significant sums to get there, and failure simply wasn't an option.

As part of the internship, we worked in a nursing home, caring for elderly patients, many of whom were either confused or agitated. The workload was intense, emotionally and physically, and we were thrown into the deep end fast. But we survived, buoyed by grit, caffeine, and late-night pep talks that often ended with laughter.

When the CAP was over, I was lucky enough to find work and begin at Palmerston North Hospital, transitioning from a student visa to a work visa. A monumental relief. The pressure of being sent back to the Philippines lifted off my shoulders.

Despite my training at St. Luke's, the hospital felt like another planet. You're not just navigating a new healthcare system; you're navigating a new culture. Kiwi patients were polite, but direct. Colleagues were warm, but expected you to pull your weight without fanfare. You learned quickly. Not just the clinical protocols, but how to laugh at yourself when you mistook *'scones'* for *'scans'* and wondered why the kitchen was involved.

Being my first foray as an Overseas Filipino Worker, the Filipino community was my lighthouse. Filipinos help each other instinctively. We're seasoned in making families out of strangers. Alynne and I later met Gibe, and we all ended up living in Kuya Alvin's house. Through him, we met Elena, Kuya Tony, Charlene, Ate Olive, and others who became our surrogate family, swapping stories over *sinigang*, hosting karaoke nights, and bringing warmth into cold Kiwi evenings.

Still, I had to repay my loan. Which meant learning to bike to work in the middle of winter, wrapped in layers, with fingers frozen stiff around the handlebars, and groceries dangling like makeshift saddlebags. It wasn't glamorous, but it was empowering. Learning to bike as an adult is humbling, but the sense of independence was unmatched.

One morning, the sky was gunmetal gray. The rain came sideways, slapping. The wind howled like it had something personal to say. My hands, numb through my gloves, trembled around the handlebars. I stood at the edge of the road, staring at the hill that curved upward toward the hospital, half-drenched, teeth clacking like castanets. A part of me whispered, *"Call in sick. Just this once."* Another part, the one forged by Tatay's 5 a.m. wake-up calls and Nanay's ironed uniforms, muttered, *"You didn't come all this way to flinch."*

So I pedaled. Slow, teeth gritted, groceries bouncing, wind pushing back like a dare. Cars splashed past, and I blinked through mist and resolve. It wasn't heroic. It was soaked, shivering, ridiculous. But it was mine. That ride — clumsy, wet, determined — was the first time I understood that courage isn't necessarily the absence of difficulty. It's the decision to keep pedaling anyway.

Then came snow. My first real snowfall, and it felt like magic. Each flake danced as it fell, the world momentarily hushed, dressed in white. I caught one on my glove and watched it melt, its brief shimmer reminding me that beauty doesn't have to last to be powerful.

Later, after paying off the loans, I bought my first car. A second-hand Honda with more personality than paint left. With the help of my friends Benjie, Jerjen, Cath, and Ian, I learned to drive. In the Philippines, owning a car was a luxury reserved for the well-off. But here, it felt achievable, almost ordinary. And yet for me, it was extraordinary. That car gave me freedom (and a working heater) and I took to the roads like someone reclaiming lost time.

I met new friends and began to feel the contours of comfort in a place that had once been completely foreign. It crept in slowly. In the routine of brunches after night shifts, in walks under cloud-swept skies, in conversations over warm tea, and in the shared silence of people who understood what it meant to start again.

And yet, for all the familiar comforts, I was also learning to be alone in the best possible way. I had time to think. To read. To run. To wonder. It was in New Zealand that I first understood what it meant to breathe without chasing the next to-do list.

Professionally, it was a step up. I gained more confidence. I stopped feeling like I had to prove something to everyone. Personally, I was beginning to unravel. The pressure to be perfect gave way to the permission to just *be*.

It wasn't all Lord of the Rings scenery and smooth sailing, of course. There were lonely nights. There were awkward conversations where I pretended to understand the Kiwi accent while silently Googling what *"Sweet as!"* meant. There was homesickness, the kind that creeps in when you see family and friends on Facebook at 2 a.m.

There were nights I wondered if I had made a mistake trading one kind of difficulty for another. The silence was beautiful, yes, but also echoey. Unforgiving. But it was in that hollowness that something stirred — the sound of my inner strength.

And there was also growth. Immense, irreversible, soul-deep. I was no longer just reacting to life. I was designing it. Slowly, gently, courageously.

The Kiwi culture taught me that courage sometimes sounds like your own breath, finally steady after a struggle. Sometimes, it looks like starting over — alone, but not afraid. It doesn't always show up with banners. Instead, it clocks in peacefully, gets back on the bike, and keeps going.

New Zealand gave me skies wide enough to dream under. More importantly, it gave me space to become quiet, and in that quiet, brave. And under those wide Kiwi skies, I learned to stand still, and still stand.

It began with a *"Kia Ora!"*. A greeting, yes, but also an invitation to become someone new. And somehow, I did.

Soul Notes

❖ When in your life have you felt most alone and yet, most yourself?

❖ What opens up in you when you stop performing and start simply being?

Chapter 6: The Land of the Long White Cloud

"He iti hoki te mokoroa nāna i kakati te kahikatea." ("Even the small worm can gnaw through the mighty kahikatea tree.")
— Māori proverb

There are places so still, they let you hear yourself again. New Zealand insisted that I meet the wild not as labor, but as invitation.

I didn't grow up camping. In Gubatan, nature wasn't an escape. It was work. It was duty. It was the earth under your father's boots, the mud between your toes while hauling crops, the sun that punished as much as it blessed. Nature was never recreational. It was where you toiled. Not where you healed.

The idea of walking through forests for fun, sleeping in tents with strangers, or carrying a stove smaller than your shoe? That was a foreign concept.

And yet — New Zealand.
Aotearoa, as the Māori call it. The Land of the Long White Cloud.

Legend has it, early Polynesian navigators spotted a long, pale cloud stretched over the horizon and knew land was near. It wasn't just a meteorological omen. It was a promise. That beneath all that sky, something was waiting — soft, solid, real. Maybe that's why I came too.

New Zealand began with a plane ride, a stranger's kindness, and the courage it took to start over. Palmerston North was my landing. All nerves, paperwork, and wide-eyed wonder. But soon, I found myself falling in love with this country.

The Great Walks came after the dust had settled. When the visas were stamped, the uniforms hung dry, and I had to learn not just how to work here, but how to *be* here. What began as migration slowly became meditation.

I was already in the country, after all. Already under the skies of *Aotearoa*. So why not walk beneath them? Why not lean into the gift of geography and let the land do what it's always done for wanderers?

The Great Walks are New Zealand's finest trails. A curated collection of tracks that take you through glaciers, beaches, volcanoes, and forest canopies. They're less about speed but more about reverence. A chance to trace the contours of a country that had, somehow, become part of my own. I hadn't planned to fall in love with New Zealand's wilderness. But once I did, I couldn't stop walking.

It began serenely. A borrowed backpack, a poorly packed lunch, someone else's tent. Just a weekend. Just a stroll. But those hills had other plans. Soon, I was chasing trailheads like answers. Reading DOC maps like scripture.

I found myself drawn to the wild the way a moth is drawn to fire. Not for danger, but for truth. In a life filled with deadlines, alarms, and fluorescent lights, the bush was one of the few places where I felt *real*. Fully present. Stripped of roles. Unmade and remade by sky and moss.

The Kepler Track was my first Great Walk. A thunderous, cinematic entry into the world of alpine dreaming. I remember the climb through the beech forest, the sound of boots squelching in mud, the golden tussock stretching far into the distance as if nature itself was exhaling. I remember my first real sunburn. I was so busy admiring the beauty, I forgot I was basically hiking on a postcard, under a hole in the ozone layer. Let's just say the views weren't the only thing glowing by sunset.

When I reached Luxmore Hut, the wind howled like it was practicing for a storm. I stood outside, jacket zipped up to my ears, watching the lake glisten below. I felt small and grateful for it. I remember crying on a rock once, not because I was hurt, but because for the first time, I realized I was safe. Not just in the trail, but in my own skin (although slightly crispier than before).

In New Zealand, access to trails is a right and not just a luxury. This country protects its wild not for the wealthy, but for everyone. There's power in that. In the Philippines, open land often meant ownership. Here, it meant belonging. No entrance fee. No gatekeeper. Just track markers and a calm sense that the land wasn't asking who you were. Only whether you'd walk gently.

And the wild waited. Still, vast, and utterly indifferent to whether I deserved it.

Routeburn was next. If Kepler was a storm, Routeburn was a poem. Waterfalls cascading like silk ribbons, valleys carved by time, swing bridges swaying above rivers that sang in glacial tones. I remember cooking instant noodles while fog crept through the trees like a sleepy giant. I remember waking up early, my hands numb, my nose cold, my heart warm. That trail taught me that solitude doesn't have to be lonely.

Then came Tongariro Northern Circuit. A Mars-like scape with sulphur in the air and mythology underfoot. Jagged rocks, ancient lava flows, the emerald shimmer of the lakes. The air carried sulphur and memory. Mount Ngauruhoe (aka Mount Doom, if you're a Lord of the Rings tragic like me) loomed, volcanic and impossible. Every step around it felt like tracing ancient fire. I was sunburnt, sore, and possibly dehydrated, but I had never felt more alive. I used to chase milestones. Out here, I followed markers. And somehow, they led me deeper into myself.

In Palmerston North, I unpacked a suitcase. In Tongariro, I unpacked something else. The parts of me that didn't yet have names, just instincts. Same journey, different luggage.

There was more trail to tread. Both outside and in.
I was changing — one ridge, one blister, one breath at a time.

One morning in Abel Tasman, I woke to *tui* birds harmonizing like a barbershop quartet that only knew one note. Another morning, it was sand in my ears and a sunrise so golden it looked photoshopped. Nature didn't care how I slept. She just showed up — unapologetic, stunning, and, occasionally, noisy.

In the middle of the walk, my blisters had blisters. At one point, I was limping so dramatically, my Osprey pack felt smug. Like it was judging me for being more *'adventure-ready'* than its owner. Stylish shoes. Terrible idea.

Heaphy Track was a masterclass in contrast. Lush rainforests, rolling tussock, and dramatic coastlines stitched together by silence that felt ancestral. Beautiful as it was, the wild had its own tests. My back ached. My legs staged a protest. I didn't think I could make it past the halfway hut. But there's something about walking through land that doesn't ask for your résumé. It just asks that you keep going.

Good thing this was New Zealand, not Australia. Sandflies and my own self-doubt were the worst that I had to fend off. No snakes, no spiders. Only my Osprey pack whispering, *"I told you so,"* and a growing awareness that this silence was the point.

With every walk, I became less about doing and more about being. I had thought reinvention came from paperwork and willpower. From visas, degrees, and grit. But each hike revealed that courage is a slow surrender. A calm arrival. The moment you walk far enough to meet the version of yourself who no longer needs to prove anything.

Lake Waikaremoana was mist and mystery. The lake itself seemed to hold stories. Ancient, sacred ones. The trail weaved through dense forest where sunlight came in beams and birdsong echoed like memory.

I walked beside her shores slowly, reverently. Not just because my back hurt, but because even the *kea* seemed to stare like nature's fashion police, judging my squeaky new boots. I walked as if the lake had something to say and I needed to be hush enough to hear it. Some trails change your pace. This one changed my pulse.

And somewhere in that rhythm — boots against dirt, breath against silence — I found parts of myself I hadn't met yet.

Let's be clear. I was no Bear Grylls. My idea of wilderness prep was Googling *"How to boil eggs with a headlamp on."* I once brought five granola bars and no spoon. I mistook a *weka* for a baby dinosaur and genuinely considered offering it my passport. But somehow, the land forgave my urban incompetence. That's the thing about nature. It lets you start messy and still rewards you with magic.

Nature doesn't hurry. And yet, everything gets done. She teaches by presence, not proclamation. In a world obsessed with optimization and hustle, the bush offered a counter-sermon. Be still. Be real. Be enough, as you are. The mountain doesn't measure your worth by how fast you climb it. Only that you show up with respect.

Camping taught me that survival isn't gritted teeth — it's peace. Not muscle, but rhythm. Not noise, but trust. It's the joy of boiled coffee at sunrise. The intimacy of silence shared between strangers in bunk beds. The freedom of walking all day without once looking at your phone.

In a world that rewards noise, the wild asked me to whisper. The Great Walks weren't just recreation. They were pilgrimage. Each summit and saddle, a prayer. Each sore muscle, an offering. More than trails, they were thresholds. With every switchback, every blisters-earned view, every whisper of wind through alpine grass, I became more. More grounded. More present. More in tune with a planet that, despite all our noise, still offers peace.

I came back from those walks smelling of smoke, covered in sweat and salt and soil, but cleaner than ever. Something in me had been reset. Like a compass realigned.

Because when you let the earth breathe back — when you let her speak through wind, stone, water, and bird — you don't just hear her. You hear *yourself*. The version of you that isn't striving, performing, or pretending. Just being. Rooted. Real.

That's the version I wanted to carry into the next chapter of my life. Into the ICU, into leadership, into the lives I would care for.

The stillness of those paths had prepared me for what was to come. It taught me how to listen. Not just to wind and trees, but to myself. I would soon learn how to hold space for others the way the mountains held space for me.

What I hadn't realized yet was that *nature* had been teaching me *courage* all along. Just not in the ways I was used to. At first glance, they couldn't have been more different. But step after step, I saw how they align.

Nature doesn't roar its bravery; it stands steady.
A tree bends but doesn't break.

Courage is choosing to return. Even when you're blistered, alone, and unsure. It's walking into silence and staying there long enough to hear the strength of your beating heart.

That long white cloud — the one ancient voyagers once followed — wasn't just above me anymore. It was *in* me now. Not fixed like the Northern Star, but subtler — Southern. More like the *Aurora Australis*. Calm, elusive, and only visible if you're paying attention.

Those wild New Zealand nights, where my only deadlines were sunsets and my only alarms were birdsong, were training me for something else. For the ICU buzz. For the weight of other people's pain. For the long nights ahead when nature's silence would be replaced by beeping machines and breathless prayers.

The mountains taught me how to listen.
The Great Walks taught me how to endure.

And when the skies cleared and the city lights returned, I was ready to walk into scrubs. Steadier, surer, and somehow still carrying the forest with me.

Soul Notes

❖ When did silence offer more comfort than company and why?

❖ What part of you emerged only when the world (or your world) went quiet?

Chapter 7: Winds, Whānau, and the Art of Care

Some places shape your profession. Others shape your soul.

Wellington did both. Between the unpredictable winds and the steady pulse of the ICU, I learned that true care is an art. A choreography of presence, precision, and heart. And in the middle of that whirlwind, I found *whānau*. Not just the patients and their families, but the colleagues who helped me refine my practice and remind me that excellence, like love, is always in the details.

In 2012, I met the soul of intensive care at the Wellington Regional Hospital. The ICU didn't just hum. It thundered. With life and death. With adrenaline and calm. With possibility and with limit. The 18-bed unit handled trauma, neuro, cardiovascular, and general intensive care. It was a world where a patient could undergo open-heart surgery one day and walk the next. Miracles and mortality, side by side.

There was magic in it. A patient sitting up after bypass, the hesitant smile of someone freshly extubated. A hand that trembled, then steadied, as a stroke patient learned to grip again. They weren't just milestones, but resurrections. I never got used to it. And I hope I never will.

But not everyone left. Some were being palliated. When medicine reached its limits. New Zealand, being a family-oriented society with strong Māori influence, approached these moments with a beautiful depth of respect. Family, or *whānau*, were central to decision-making. Family meetings, led by the ICU consultant, were often heavy with emotion. Yet they were also profound. We spoke of afterlife beliefs, spiritual readiness, and sometimes, the gift of organ donation.

Around that time, I began learning more about the Treaty of Waitangi, the foundational agreement between the Crown and Māori. It wasn't a relic of the past. It was a living covenant shaping New Zealand's laws, language, and spirit.

For someone who loved law and lived with the colonial scars of the Philippines, it gave me hope. Here was a country where indigenous and white communities were not perfect, but striving — openly, structurally, respectfully — to walk together. It lit up my sense of justice and showed me what equity could look like when it was baked into the national soul. The world could learn something from *Aotearoa*.

These conversations taught me that life and death, when approached with compassion and clarity, could be a bridge to healing.

What struck me most was how closely the *whānau* dynamic mirrored Filipino values. The same collective strength. The same reverence for elders. The same instinct to gather, to cook, to stay by the bedside. Not out of duty, but out of love. Watching Māori families encircle their sick with *karakia*, stories, and silence felt achingly familiar. Like echoes of home in a different accent.

In the unit, I was mentored by Kris, a fellow Filipino nurse and self-proclaimed perfectionist. But Kris didn't micromanage; he mentored. He taught through example, through gentle correction, through a kind of relentless steadiness. He insisted on the little things. Cords never left on the floor, the syringes and aliquots of normal saline in the stock trolley perfectly aligned, bedsheets tucked with military precision, oral and eye care — frequent and thorough. What may seem like hospital etiquette to some was, to him, and eventually to me, a discipline of excellence.

Outside the hospital, Kris was a celebrated artist. A painter of horizons, with works that carried the weight of silence and depth. His attention to detail in art mirrored his discipline at work. It made sense. Care, after all, is an artform.

I loved the challenge. I was hungry to learn. And under his tutelage, I didn't just become a better nurse. I became someone who noticed, who refined, who took pride in the smallest details.

It was also in Wellington where I reconnected with my college friend Anne, who had recommended the ICU role to me. That single suggestion became a turning point. With her, Kris, and fellow ICU rookies — Pam, Kryslene, and Diana — we were tossed into the deep end. Ventilators, vasopressors, and acronyms that sounded like encrypted spells. We laughed through the chaos, mispronounced drug names, and once accidentally used a ventilator tube as a headband mid-simulation. We had no choice but to learn fast. And we did, together.

Wellington itself? A character of its own. Perched between hills and harbor on the southern tip of New Zealand's North Island, it's the capital city also known as *'Windy Welly'*. And rightfully so. It could blow your umbrella inside out, toss your scarf into the sea, and ruin your hair before shift change.

But oh, when it was beautiful, it was unbeatable. I remember sitting by the Oriental Bay, munching on fish and chips, watching dolphins leap across the water like exclamation marks written by the sea. Joyful, fleeting, and unforgettable.

Kiwis have a thing for comfort and discreet delight. Flat whites served with a smile, *pavlova* debated like scripture, cinema embraced like sacred ritual. I was lucky enough to be there for the parade of stars during *The Hobbit* premiere. The whole city dressed up — elf ears, capes, costumes — and it felt like watching a small nation write itself into myth, one pointed ear and one poetic flourish at a time.

There's something disarming about New Zealand. The sincerity. The softness. The way even its caffeine feels like a hug. But across the Tasman, Australia is always watching. And eventually, just like it claimed the flat white and the *pavlova*, Australia would steal me too.

Wellington had a way of rewarding you. After a hard shift, after a hard week. With just enough magic to keep you going.

Life in that city, in that unit, shaped me. It was there I learned that ICU isn't just about saving lives. It's about honoring them. In the care you give, the standards you uphold, and the grace with which you face both triumph and farewell.

The winds of Wellington may have been wild, but they taught me steadiness. *Whānau* taught me how to hold space for others. And let them hold space for me.

And the true art of nursing? That wasn't in the textbooks. It was in the way Kris arranged the linen, the way a patient whispered thank you with their eyes, the way we all stood still when a life slipped away. It wasn't just nursing. It was reverence. And I carry it still.

New Zealand, in many ways, was *paradise*. A country of fairness, breathtaking beauty, and calm brilliance.

As much as I loved it, I couldn't stay. Not because something was wrong, but because something else was calling. Somewhere else needed the nurse I had become, and the human I was still uncovering. I couldn't name it yet, but I felt it. That pull toward something more global, more complex, more... *unfinished.*

Also, let's be honest. It was cold. I missed the kind of sun that seeps into your bones — not just your jacket.

Soul Notes

❖ Who pushed you to grow without pulling you apart?

❖ What place taught you something you didn't expect and didn't know you needed?

❖ Who taught you that attention is a form of love and how did they show it?

Chapter 8: G'day Mate: The Audacity of Starting Again

The audacity to start again will rarely be met with applause. More often, it's met with resistance. From systems, from circumstance, from the voices in your head asking,
Who do you think you are?
You were already in New Zealand. Why want more?

Australia didn't begin with a bang. It began with bureaucracy.

Forms. Stacks of them. I had to convince AHPRA, the Australian Health Practitioner Regulation Authority, to recognize every qualification and credential I'd earned as a nurse. Academic transcripts, licensure verifications, references from supervisors who had long since changed email addresses. Every document had to be meticulously gathered, notarized, uploaded, often more than once.

At the same time, the Department of Home Affairs demanded immigration clearances and criminal history checks from every country I'd lived in. A paper trail through nations. Each form needed another form to explain it. Every signature needed a witness. Every upload had a deadline and a glitch. Even getting Wi-Fi felt like a bureaucratic triathlon. Email confirmations, identity verifications, passwords scribbled on the back of receipts already covered in conversion rates and grocery math.

It was a *trial by paperwork,* a rite of passage that people born in the *right* country might never fully understand. For them, legitimacy is assumed. For us, it must be proven. Relentlessly, exhaustively, in duplicate.

But that's where my audacity came in. I knew it would be uphill. I chose it anyway. The willingness to start again — not because I had to, but because I dared to — is its own kind of courage. It's the kind that doesn't bark but prints syllabi between shifts. It calls embassies on lunch breaks. It keeps going, even when no one's cheering.

My move to Queensland in 2014 felt less like stepping into a new chapter and more like trying to reboot a life on dial-up.

But then, slowly, the static cleared. And I looked up.

The skies stretched wide and cinematic. The kind of blue that made you squint, as if God had gotten carried away with the saturation slider. The air smelled of eucalyptus and sun-warmed concrete. The buses ran on time. People greeted you *"G'day!"* and called you *'mate'* without irony.

There was a rhythm here. Casual but not careless, warm without being intrusive, unhurried but efficient. And once I stopped trying to outpace it, I began to match it. Australia wasn't a place to land; it was a place to rebuild. It didn't demand a résumé at first glance. It gave you space to arrive.

I started at Gold Coast University Hospital. Brand new, gleaming, like a futuristic LEGO set assembled with clinical precision and fluorescent ambition.

A year later, I transferred to the Royal Brisbane and Women's Hospital. More pace, more polish, more tea breaks. Aussies, I quickly learned, take their tea more seriously than their politicians.

I had to relearn not just procedures, but language. *'Brekkie'* meant breakfast. *"Yeah, nah"* was a full sentence. *"Nah, yeah"* meant something else entirely. The culture shock didn't hit like a slap, it seeped in, one slang term at a time.

Every hospital has its own rhythm, and I was the new guy again hoping not to press the wrong button on the vitals monitor. But I found my footing. I brought with me Filipino empathy, Kiwi resilience, and slowly grafted it onto Aussie pragmatism. I wasn't just surviving anymore. I was syncing. Building a new version of myself. One shift, one cup of tea at a time.

Then (because apparently full-time nursing wasn't chaotic enough), I enrolled in law school.

No one asked me to do this. No tragic courtroom origin story. No wise mentor whispering *"You'd make a great lawyer."* Just a persistent, inner nudge. The kind that only shows up once your life gets silent enough for you to hear yourself think: *What else?*

Law school had always been there, tucked behind the curtain of my *'practical'* career choices. A haunting, a dare, a song I knew all the words to but had never dared to sing out loud.

Nursing gave me certainty. Law gave me possibility.

I worried I was too old. Too brown. Too visibly different in a lecture hall filled with people who could quote Blackstone like sports stats. I feared becoming the token student in every diversity photo. Some days, I felt like a guest in a house I'd never been invited to — nodding along, translating in my head, praying the impostor syndrome wasn't audible.

But fear, I've learned, isn't the enemy. It's the usher that walks you to the threshold of the life you secretly want.

So, in 2015, I enrolled at QUT — Queensland University of Technology — in Brisbane. Partly because it was close, partly because it had a solid reputation, and mostly because my budget didn't allow for existential dithering.

The campus sat in the heart of the city, wedged between old parliament buildings and the botanic gardens, where the air always carried a mix of eucalyptus, ambition, and overpriced flat whites.

A few years earlier, I'd been sipping flat whites in Wellington, where even the milk felt gentler. There, the *pavlova* was debated like scripture. Here, in Brisbane, it was devoured with cheeky certainty. Australia hadn't invented the flat white or *pavlova*, but it had claimed them, casually and confidently, as if it always had. And in its own way, it was starting to do the same with me.

I was beginning to understand that countries don't always embrace you with ceremony. Sometimes, they absorb you. Through their commutes, their slang, their coffee rituals, until one day, without fanfare, you realize you belong to them. Stubbornly. Almost accidentally.

QUT's law library had those monolithic tomes. The kind that seemed to sneer if you mispronounced *'tort.'* It was loud and quiet all at once. Intimidating and exhilarating. A pressure cooker of caffeine, competition, and potential. It was exactly where I needed to be.

Balancing work and study was chaos, but the structured kind. I'd chart vitals by day and analyze High Court rulings by night. Sometimes I'd confuse the two, nearly writing *'administer IV fluids'* in the margin of my Corporations Law textbook.

I wasn't sleeping much. My social life became a myth, a legend from pre-law school times. But I didn't mind. Because something had clicked.

I wasn't leaving nursing behind. I was expanding the toolkit. Nursing gave me proximity to suffering. Law gave me the framework to interrogate it. I didn't just want to manage systems. I wanted to change them.

The transformation didn't arrive with trumpets. It crawled in, weary, stubborn, unpaid. There were days I questioned everything. Like the night I worked an ICU double shift, came home, and tried to read a 35-page judgment on constitutional interpretation. I gave up, stared at the ceiling, and considered whether I should instead pursue a less stressful goal. Like becoming a monk. Or a barista in Bali.

It was madness.

But then, I'd remember why I was doing this. Not to impress. Not even to prove anything. But to build something. To integrate my past selves into a future I could call *mine.*

I wasn't chasing prestige. I wasn't even sure I'd pass. But something in me, stubborn, tired, alive, needed to know I could try. To see what kind of man I could become if I didn't play it safe. If I let ambition and not just duty steer the wheel.

That's the thing about reinvention. It's rarely dramatic. Sometimes, it looks like signing up for a course no one else sees coming. Choosing curiosity over comfort. Starting again not because you're lost, but because you've grown.

Queensland wasn't just the backdrop for this shift. It was the incubator. It let me evolve. From *What do I want to be?* to *What can I contribute?* I wasn't just a nurse. Or a law student. Or a migrant trying to blend in. I was all those things. Dynamic and multi-layered.

Looking back, I didn't always recognize the transformation while it was happening. It wasn't a single decision or dramatic turning point. It was dozens of small choices stacked on top of each other. One shift. One reading. One risk. And somehow, through the exhaustion and essays and exams, I had begun again. Not by abandoning who I was, but by daring to evolve who I could become.

Starting again made me let go of neat narratives and embrace the mess of reinvention. To accept that progress sometimes looks like exhaustion, that clarity may arrive only after chaos, and that courage often wears the face of stubborn, unglamorous persistence.

If Queensland taught me anything, it's this:
Starting again isn't a detour.
It's the conviction that there's more to give, more to build, more to become.

And even as I found my footing in this new version of myself — nurse, law student, new Australian — I sensed the story wasn't done. Reinvention rarely ends with closure. It stirs restlessness. It plants seeds. And before you know it, that unrest becomes a rhythm. A drumbeat, a call to motion.

What began with flat whites and footnotes in Brisbane was no longer just a chapter. It was momentum. Once you begin again, you also remember how to move, forward and with fire. Toward something braver. Something louder. Something like… *Vamos.*

Soul Notes

❖ What dream have you shelved because it didn't 'fit' the version of you others recognize?

❖ When did you act boldly, not out of obligation, but because something in you refused to shrink?

❖ Are you building a life that reflects your full self or just the version that fits the résumé?

Chapter 9: Vamos

Before I became a lawyer, before I found my footing in immigration law or stood in front of a room holding space with my words, I was another newcomer to Australia. Fresh off the plane, exhilarated and exposed.

In those early days, I was rebuilding — piece by piece in the corners of Queensland. I juggled a flat white and a textbook, stitching together two callings that rarely belonged in the same sentence.

That season wasn't glamorous. But it taught me how to start again without waiting for permission. And soon, I would learn how to move. Toward something, and with it.

I thought momentum would be my medicine. That if I kept doing — studying, working, proving — I could outpace whatever was unsettled inside me. I'd eventually arrive somewhere that felt like home. The sun blazed, the beaches sparkled, and everything looked like progress. But beneath it all, I was restless. Fragmented. Living a life that advanced, but didn't yet feel like mine.

I didn't know it then, but *Vamos* would become my anchor. Not just a word, but a worldview. A rhythm I'd return to in moments of doubt, fatigue, and reinvention.

I loved the Gold Coast. The sun was unrelenting. The beaches — Tallebudgera, Burleigh Heads, Snapper Rocks — glimmered like postcards. The skies felt infinite. The breeze carried sunscreen, sea salt, and ambition. But even in all that radiance, something inside me stayed dim.

Something was missing.

Myself.

Back then, I hadn't named all the parts of me yet. The nurse who could care with clinical precision, the future lawyer learning how to fight, the achiever chasing progress, the young man trying to find his way in the world. The part of me trained to heal others didn't know how to tend to the ache within. But I could feel them pulling in different directions. I could be competent enough. But I couldn't feel whole. *Yet.*

Australia was stunning, but for someone like me — hungry for meaning, for resonance, for a way to be fully seen — it often felt frustratingly surface-level. People were kind. Polite. But finding kindred spirits — people who wrestled with ideas, who spoke in metaphors, who lived in translation — felt like trying to catch smoke.

I told myself I should be grateful. Thanks to the mobility of nursing, I arrived with an immigrant visa in hand. A headstart most don't get. I was enrolled in a post-graduate nursing program, working hospital shifts, getting paid decently and praised for efficiency. On paper, it was progress.

But comfort, I would learn, can be a paradox. It numbs as much as it nourishes. Progress without purpose starts to feel like a cage lined with compliments. One night, after another long shift and microwaved dinner, I played *She Used to Be Mine* on loop from the musical *Waitress*. Not because I liked being sad, but because the song felt like a mirror I hadn't dared to hold up. It was a ballad about losing yourself. About waking up one day and realizing the person in the mirror was someone you used to know.

Waitress wasn't just a musical. It was a mirror. A reminder that simple lives can still carry epic transformations. That a woman making pies in a diner can still be a revolutionary act, if it means choosing herself. It gave me permission to believe that even ordinary choices — saying no, walking away, reclaiming rest — could be acts of courage.

I had come to Queensland thinking I was rebuilding. But what I didn't see, until then, was how I'd slowly become a stranger to the version of myself who once believed becoming more didn't have to mean becoming unrecognizable.

It was a strange kind of disorientation. Doing all the right things, in the right place, with the right credentials, yet feeling like a ghost inside my own story. The more I achieved, the more invisible I became to myself. I didn't have a name for that ache back then. Only a grief for a self I couldn't seem to find.

But I wasn't just looking for a livelihood. I was looking for a life. And in the silence between shifts, I felt the loneliness not of being alone, but of being unanchored. That ache demanded more than comfort. It needed expression. So, I looked for a space where I could speak. Even if my voice still shook.

I tried the usual avenues. Nursing conferences, community groups, church functions. I even volunteered for events I didn't care about just to feel proximity to people. But nothing clicked. I didn't just want company. I wanted connection.

Then one day, while wandering the streets of Southport, I noticed a cluster of people entering a building. A small sign greeted me: *Toastmasters International.* At first glance, it sounded like something for real estate agents and reluctant best men or a support group for PowerPoint enthusiasts. But something — maybe boredom, maybe hope — nudged me inside.

What I didn't know then was that this small decision — to follow a group of strangers into a room — would become a hinge moment. An unplanned yes that would echo across years and continents.

Toastmasters International is where introverts go to suffer and extroverts go to humble-brag, all in three-minute speeches. A structured space that walks a tightrope between hilarity and heartache. From hilarious icebreakers to heartbreakingly raw truths. Complete with printed agendas, timekeepers, and just a little too much eye contact. And applause? Relentless. Even the guy who called his boss '*mum*' during Table Topics got a standing ovation. (Truly, a hero.)

So, I joined.

And I kept coming back.

It was a decision that, in hindsight, shaped everything that came next. Southport Toastmasters became my first real community in Australia. Argentine Daniel, Australian Daniel, Roy, Pat, Valerie, Paula, Michelle, Lloydie, Alisha — a hodgepodge of locals and global wanderers who gathered weekly not just to improve their public speaking, but to listen. Really listen. That was new to me. And from that listening, I began to find my voice.

Back then, I was still shy. This was pre-law, pre-bar exam, pre-everything. But something inside me was stirring. Every time I got up to speak, I chipped away at the idea that my voice wasn't enough. Toastmasters became my rehearsal room for courage.

And then I met Mark Hunter. The 2009 Toastmasters world champion of public speaking, he didn't just tweak my speech, he cracked something open.

When I shared the first draft of a speech I wrote called *"Vamos"*, he didn't nod politely. He leaned forward and said, *"You've lived this. Now speak it like you mean it."* I learned to own the story. To speak not just to impress, but to connect. That speech would later travel with me, in spirit, across oceans.

Vamos! — the rallying cry of Rafael Nadal — is a word I've long carried with me, not just as a fan of tennis, but as a believer in relentless motion. In Spanish, it means *"Let's go!"*, but it's more than that. It's about momentum. Forward motion. Drive. It's what you say when your legs are heavy, and your heart is tired, but the finish line still demands your best.

Vamos is the defiance of stagnation. The whisper that becomes a war cry when things get hard. It's a mindset. A mentality. A decision to get up, show up, and push forward.

Toastmasters helped me find my voice. But courage didn't stop at speaking. It needed movement. And that's where Nadal — and *Vamos* — found me.

In 2014, I watched Nadal live in the semifinals of the Australian Open, battling Federer in a match that gripped the entire crowd. Rod Laver Arena buzzed with a nervous electricity. A heatwave of bodies and adrenaline. The court glowed an impossible shade of blue, like the surface of a glacial lake under floodlights. Flags waved. Beers foamed. Sunscreen lingered in the air despite the night setting in. Above it all, the sound. A swell of gasps, claps, and collective exhales.

Swiss Federer moved like elegance personified — smooth, efficient, seemingly untouched by effort. Spanish Nadal, by contrast, played like a storm breaking through the baseline — gritty, relentless, muscles taut with defiance. Where Federer floated, Nadal fought.

Every time Nadal faced a break point, every time his back was against the wall, he would bellow: *"Vamos!"* With each shout, the crowd leaned in. He wasn't just playing tennis; he was summoning courage. The cry bounced off the rafters and into our chests. He won that match in four gritty sets but lost the final to another Swiss player Stan Wawrinka. And yet, that loss didn't diminish the meaning of *Vamos*. It deepened it. Because *Vamos* isn't about perfection. It's about persistence.

Years later, I would find myself in Paris — not as a tourist, but as a resident, threading through *Métro* lines and *boulangeries* like I belonged. Every May, I made my pilgrimage to Roland-Garros for the French Open. It became a ritual — part nostalgia, part reverence. And each year, I watched Rafael Nadal command the clay courts with the same fire that first etched the word *Vamos* into my bones.

He won there fourteen times. A near-mythic reign on clay. In Paris, where elegance often trumps passion, Nadal was worshipped. A monument stands in his name. Proof that grit earns reverence. The crowd still cried out *Allez!*, but when Nadal played, you'd hear something else rise from the stands: *Vamos!*

Amid the noise of the battle cries, something clicked. *Vamos* was no longer just a Spanish word. It had become a philosophy. A call to move forward despite fear. A commitment to risk, to fall, and to stand up again.

In my life, *Vamos* had become a mantra. A mental armor I adopted for life. When people questioned my pace, I focused on direction. When self-doubt whispered, I answered with discipline. When life overwhelmed me, I whispered back: *Vamos*.

In 2015, I channeled that energy into something equally punishing. The Gold Coast Marathon. I remember preparing for it like it was my ticket to proving that I could conquer the world. By then, I was in law school, working full-time as an ICU nurse, and still clinging to the last scraps of energy I had left to chase big dreams.

I trained for months. Early mornings. Miles on end. Sore knees. Blistered feet. My entire life was study, shift, run, repeat. On the day of the race, despite all that preparation, the road hit back. It was long. The sun was brutal. My legs screamed to stop. But I didn't. I couldn't.

It wasn't a whisper anymore. It was muscle memory.

Kilometre after kilometre, I ran with grit.
Not triumphantly, but honestly.

When my lungs begged for mercy. When my thoughts turned treacherous. When the sun blazed down like an unforgiving spotlight. When the crowd cheers dulled and all I had was my own inner voice, raspy and relentless. It got me across the finish line. Because *Vamos* isn't about conquering with style. It's about finding your reservoir of strength and refusing to surrender.

And that mentality followed me into law school. Every 12-hour hospital shift followed by a five-hour study session was a small act of rebellion against exhaustion. Every late night with torts or contracts or constitutional law was a moment I chose direction over doubt. I wasn't born rich, brilliant, or well-connected. But I kept going. I kept whispering that I am the grittiest. *Vamos*!

Nadal showed me how to trust its power.

In 2022, I visited Manacor, a small town on the island of Mallorca, Spain, marvelled at the same streets he walked, and saw the Rafa Nadal Academy, a cathedral of perseverance and training ground of future tennis superstars, including Alexa Eala, rising tennis star and first Filipina to enter the WTA Top 100.

Rafa Nadal's journey from his humble beginnings in Manacor resonated with me. Like mine in Gubatan. Manacor, a place where grit is carved into clay courts and sweaty t-shirts, where Nadal first picked up a racquet and began shaping his destiny.

Standing at the gates of the Rafa Nadal Academy, I didn't feel like a tourist. I was a pilgrim carrying not a camera, but a question: *What does it mean to keep showing up?*

In that space carved by sweat and spirit, I thought of every immigrant, every outsider, every dreamer. I am reminded that *Vamos* is what my family embodied in their sacrifices. What every immigrant chants silently with each visa application. What I tell my clients, my mentees, my patients, and sometimes, even strangers.

Even now, as a lawyer, as someone who mentors others and represents people whose dreams hang in the balance of bureaucracy, and as a nurse, who mobilizes patients after lengthy operations, I remind them: *Vamos.*

Let's go. Let's keep moving.
You're allowed to be scared. Just don't be still.

What started as a Toastmasters speech became a life philosophy. And little did I know back then, in that room in the Gold Coast, that Toastmasters would meet me again years later in Germany. That I'd find another anchor tribe in Frankfurt. That my voice, once wobbly and unsure, would stand tall across countries, courtrooms, and continents.

Toastmasters didn't just give me a stage. It gave me back my voice. Not the version shaped by hospital protocols or legalese, but something warmer. Playful. I cracked jokes again. Dared to sound like myself. Even when accent felt out of place. The voice I would carry across borders. From the Gold Coast to Germany, from uncertainty to advocacy, it reminded me that stories are bridges. And mine was worth telling.

Because that's what *Vamos* gave me: the strength to speak and the courage to keep walking with it.

So, whether you're standing on the Rod Laver Arena, sitting through an immigration interview, or just alone in a new country trying to figure out who you are and why you're there, may you find your own rally cry.

In whatever language.
Forza! Idemo! Allez! Auf geht's!
Ganbatte! Jiāyóu! Kaya mo yan! Aja aja!

In whatever volume.
Whispered in a hospital corridor or shouted into the void.

And when the day drags, your motivation is on par with a toddler's attention span, or you feel like a background character in your own story — remember: even Rafael Nadal loses the final sometimes. Doesn't stop him being Nadal.

Besides, a has-been still ran the race.
A never-was didn't even tie their shoes.

You don't have to roar. Just remember the direction.
And take one more step.

So, when in doubt?

Vamos.

—

I used to think *Vamos* meant pushing forward no matter what. That if I just kept moving, kept achieving, kept grinding, I'd arrive at certainty. Eventually, even motion needs meaning.

I'd spent so long choosing velocity over stillness, grit over gentleness. *But what if Vamos wasn't just a call to charge ahead?*

That question would follow me into my next chapter. Because soon, I would stop chasing the finish line, and instead, choose wonder. Choose detour. Choose stillness. The kind that humbles, that heals. The kind that looks like sand dunes, soft light, and surrender.

And in doing so, I'd begin to remember not just how to move — but why I started running in the first place.

Soul Notes

❖ What's your personal *Vamos* — the mantra, memory, or fire that keeps you moving?

❖ When was the last time you kept going, even when everything in you said, "Stop"?

❖ And what would it mean, not just to move, but to move on purpose?

Chapter 10: 100 Days of Summer: Postcards from a Pause

Since the Bronze Age, humans have wandered. To survive, to seek meaning. Pilgrimage, conquest, and curiosity — motions that mirror an internal search.

In the summer of 2016, I made a decision that didn't make sense on paper. I could've enrolled in extra units and inched closer to finishing law school, but something in me resisted. *Not yet. Not now.* I didn't want to finish exhausted and unsure why I'd started. I needed to remember what I was running toward.

I wanted to feel something again. Awe. Curiosity. A reason to keep going that wasn't just efficiency in disguise.

Anthony Bourdain once said, *"If I'm an advocate for anything, it's to move. As far as you can, as much as you can... across the ocean or simply across the river. Walk in someone else's shoes or at least eat their food."*

This wasn't about ticking off countries but about tasting the world, one honest bite at a time. A *pierogi* in Krakow. *Churrasco* in Rio. A diner breakfast in D.C. The food wasn't always fancy. But always real. And real was what I was hungry for.

So, I chose to travel. To say yes to a summer stitched together by global events — World Youth Day in Krakow, the Olympics in Rio, a Toastmasters conference in Washington, D.C. It wasn't the fastest route to a law degree, but it may have been the fastest route back to myself.

It started as a simple holiday. And ended up as a defining chapter in my personal legend.

Europe: Nostalgia and Friendship

The first leg was Europe, with my best friend Joan. We met our other friends Jo, Weng, Yulrich, Shishi, and Abz in London, and for a few days, the world was tea, theatre, and cobblestone magic. We wandered through Bath and the majestic halls of Windsor Castle, visited the Prime Meridian in Greenwich, and lived our childhood dreams. The kind sparked by textbooks and flashlight reading under mosquito nets.

From London, Joan and I crisscrossed the continent.

In Lisbon, we drank port, devoured *pulpo*, and ended meals with warm *pastéis de nata*.

In Paris, we appreciated art. In the museums and on the street. Everyone seemed fashionable in black.

In Barcelona, we pedaled through *Passeig de Gràcia* and met a fellow Pinoy named Bijo, a solo traveler powered by *paella* and *sangria*.

We wandered past whimsical buildings that looked like they'd been dreamed up by someone who refused straight lines. Gaudí's fingerprints were everywhere. His architecture wasn't about symmetry or logic. It was about longing. Structures curving and spiraling, as if to touch heaven sideways.

And then — the *Sagrada Família*. That unfinished cathedral rising like a hymn interrupted. Each spire jagged and reaching, each façade etched with stories in stone. It wasn't just a building. It was devotion in delay. A monument to what happens when vision outlives its architect. I stood beneath its intricate towers and thought: *Not everything needs to be finished to be revered.*

As Filipinos, we're taught to view Spanish history with suspicion. Colonizers who stamped out our languages and named our saints. But in Barcelona, as I clinked glasses with Joan and Bijo in a tapas bar echoing with laughter, I saw a strange familiarity as I watched the Spanish people. Their joy, their late dinners, their fondness for drama and devotion felt uncannily like home. It's a wild thing to recognize your colonizer's face, and realize it might also be your uncle's.

In Rome, we napped at Castel Sant'Angelo on monobloc chairs, too exhausted from a day of queuing in Musei Vaticani to care that we were sleeping in public.

And in Berlin, Joan saved me. When I was being mugged, she snatched my wallet right back. Fearless and fast. One of the toughest women I know. Funny enough, years later, we'd both end up back in Germany calling it home — Joan in Berlin, me in Frankfurt.

Of course, not everything was effortless. That summer was humid, our tempers occasionally flared, and we didn't always want the same things. I was a *'cover five cities in three days'* type; Joan wanted to savor every moment. Travel tests friendships. But the best ones bend without breaking. Real friendships transcend heat, stress, and miscommunication.

The monuments were grand, the food unforgettable, but the best part was sharing those moments with someone who had seen my dreams form before they ever took shape. Joan and I had once stood on opposite sides of school politics. Me as editor-in-chief of the college paper, her as student council president. We didn't always agree back then. Our debates were sharp, our visions clashed. But even in those years of tension, the respect never wavered. Somehow, we stayed friends.

And now, here we were — years later, thousands of miles from home — still navigating cities, stories, and each other.

Friendship had been my compass in Europe. Now, I wanted to see where solitude might take me.

Czech Republic: Existential Introspection

First stop: I arrived in Prague not sure what I was looking for. Only that something about the city had always tugged at me. Maybe it was the architecture. Part fairy tale, part fever dream. Or the literary shadow of Kafka, whose stories had taught me that absurdity and meaning often walked hand in hand. Or to be somewhere where I didn't understand the language — so I could better hear myself.

The first thing I saw was the Astronomical Clock. A medieval marvel that still ticks like it's whispering secrets to the sky. Every hour, tourists gather for the show. A mechanical parade of apostles, death with his hourglass, the rooster that crows at the end. It's over in under a minute and people still clap. I thought of it as a strange metaphor for life. We build these elaborate routines hoping someone notices, hoping it adds up to something worth applauding.

But the real magic wasn't in the clock. It was in the streets that spilled out around it, where buildings leaned in like they had stories to tell, if you just lingered a little longer. It was on Charles Bridge, where buskers played violins and accordions like incantations, their music hovering above the Vltava River like a spell. One duo sang Leonard Cohen's *Hallelujah* in Czech, and I didn't need to understand the words to feel it — that trembling mix of sorrow and surrender.

In that moment, I stopped trying to translate everything. I listened. And sometimes, you find meaning by just allowing things to unfold.

I liked Prague because it reminded me of law school. All structure
on the surface, peacefully absurd underneath. Bureaucratic rituals,
unspoken hierarchies, rules that made sense only if you stopped
asking questions. Kafka would've understood.

Austria: Elegance in Stillness

In Vienna, I slowed down. After weeks of trains, transfers, and
travel tension, the city felt like a breath held just a moment longer.
Elegant without trying, serious without scowling, Vienna had the
confidence of someone whose silence says more than most
speeches.

I wandered through Schönbrunn Palace, gold leaf and symmetry
for days, marveling at how much opulence could coexist with
order. Even the gardens seemed to exhale on beat. I sipped *melange*
at Café Central, where once, Trotsky and Freud sat just tables
apart, likely solving the world's problems over pastries.

I didn't solve anything. Just savored something that didn't need
fixing. A very good *sachertorte*. It arrived like a well-dressed diplomat
— dignified, dark, and unapologetically Austrian. You didn't just
eat it; you communed with it. A perfect triangle of bittersweet
chocolate cake, cloaked in a mirror-shine glaze that reflected the
chandelier overhead. The thin layer of apricot jam at its heart
offered a sly note of brightness, cutting through the decadence like
a waltz interrupting a funeral dirge.

It sat on a white porcelain plate edged in gold, flanked by a dollop
of unsweetened whipped cream. Not piped, not precious, just
casually spooned on like a knowing friend. Each bite tasted like
velvet and history. Cocoa and empire.

And then — the *schnitzel*. At Figlmüller Wollzeile, Vienna's temple
of fried veal. The plate arrived like a dare. The size of a steering

wheel, golden and crackling at the edges, served with a wedge of lemon and absolutely no apology.

For a few sacred minutes, I forgot the to-do lists, forgot the worries of the world, forgot the question of what came next. There was just one bite, then another, and then silence — the kind only excellent food can justify. It was everything they said it would be, and then some.

One afternoon, I stumbled into a string quartet performance at Karlskirche — Vivaldi's *Four Seasons*. I expected to be entertained. Instead, I was undone. The music moved through my chest like a memory I didn't know I had. The violins surged and softened, and I found myself blinking away tears. Maybe from beauty. Or realizing that I hadn't been still enough, long enough, to let anything truly move me.

In Vienna, stillness wasn't stagnation. It was permission.
To not rush. To not optimize. To not explain.
There, I didn't chase meaning. I simply made space for it to arrive.

Croatia: Fantasy to Grounded Solitude

Next stop: Croatia. A detour that began with a fandom fantasy but deepened into something more elemental. I drove from Zagreb to Dubrovnik, tracing a coastline so beautiful it looked photoshopped.

In Zagreb, I wandered through the Museum of Broken Relationships. A gallery of relics from heartbreaks past, each item paired with a story more piercing than the last. A wedding dress. A toaster. A love letter never sent. Oddly, it didn't feel heavy. It felt honest. A reminder that we all carry things we don't post about.

In Plitvice Lakes, waterfalls spilled like silver threads through emerald forests. I hiked alone, each footstep swallowed by moss and mist, feeling at once very small and very alive.

In Split, I sat beneath Roman arches, journal in one hand and gelato in the other, listening to the slow shuffle of tourists and the occasional laughter of strangers. It was the first time I felt no pressure to narrate the moment. Just to live it. A pause worth taking.

And then — Dubrovnik. The end of the line. The jewel of the Adriatic and the filming location for Game of Thrones' King's Landing. I stood on the stone steps where fictional kings had fallen. But what stayed with me wasn't the fantasy. It was the sunlight warming the limestone, the salt in the air, and the stillness I didn't know I'd needed.

I wasn't chasing dragons. I came to reclaim my own fire.

Poland: Spiritual Grounding

Next stop: Krakow, Poland, for World Youth Day. Picture over a million young people gathered not for a concert, but for a celebration of faith. Flags waved. Languages danced. Voices lifted in unison. We caught a glimpse of Pope Francis, and I visited the tombs of Sister Faustina and Pope John Paul II. It was reverent, electric, and grounding.

I also explored the Wieliczka Salt Mine. A vast cathedral carved from salt, glittering with chandeliers and sculpted saints. It reminded me that even beneath the surface, beauty can bloom.

Brazil: Joy through service

From Krakow, I flew to Brazil to volunteer as a nurse at the Rio 2016 Olympics. I was assigned to the equestrian events, a niche I didn't know I'd love. Our team was a medley of cultures and accents, but we all spoke the same unspoken language —

Service. Respect. Excellence.

In a world obsessed with credentials, it felt radical to contribute without being center stage.

Rio was alive. Steep hills crowned by Christ the Redeemer, the golden beaches of Ipanema and Copacabana humming with samba, and street food that could convert any skeptic. Even now, I can still taste the warmth of *pão de queijo* — doughy, golden, unapologetically comforting — and the sharp citrus bite of a cold *caipirinha*. I imagined Bourdain here, saying something silly and profound in equal measure.

During off-hours, the International Olympic Committee gifted us with tickets to events. I watched world-class athletes make magic. My favorite? Rafael Nadal. After he won the men's tennis doubles gold medal match with his compatriot Marc Lopez, I asked for a selfie, forgetting my front camera had a 10-second delay. Nadal smiled and waited. And waited. Ten long seconds, frozen in kindness. That photo isn't just a memory; it's a metaphor for grace under pressure.

I didn't wear a medal. Just a volunteer badge and standard-issue uniform. But I left with something shinier. A sense of usefulness that didn't need applause.

Ah. *Saudade* — that aching sweetness for something beautiful and gone, something you lived and now feels like both longing and love.

The Mainland U.S.: the Seed of a Dream

After Rio came Washington, D.C., where I attended the
Toastmasters World Conference. That year, Mohammed Qahtani
won the World Championship of Public Speaking with a speech
called *"The Power of Words."* His message? Words can lift people up.
Or tear them apart. That speech didn't just move the room; it
moved something inside me. I remembered why I started speaking
in the first place.

I also stayed with my sister Nora and her family in Virginia. Family
dinners, laughter, and the kind of love that reminds you where you
come from. Then, with friends Odessa and Cecille, I road-tripped
up the East Coast. In Manhattan, the skyscrapers sparked
something ambitious. In Hudson Valley, the calm whispered of
possibility.

In Boston, I walked the halls of Harvard Law. Not with envy, but
recognition. A voice inside stirred: *You belong here, too.* Not for
prestige. But because your story holds.

Then came the West Coast. First, Las Vegas, where neon ambition
lit the streets. Yosemite, where I camped alone under the stars and
stared up at Half Dome, equal parts terrified and alive. And the
Grand Canyon, a jaw-dropping reminder that some things can only
be understood through silence.

I ended in San Francisco, where the Golden Gate greeted me in a
shroud of fog. I did the tourist triad — Alcatraz, Pier 39, and that
hilariously steep street that's both cardio test and Instagram cliché.

I was with Auntie Belen, Nanay's sister. A nurse well into her 70s,
still working, still hustling. Probably had savings tucked away, but
still queuing for food stamps like it was part of her DNA. The

OFW spirit — resilient, resourceful, a little stubborn — doesn't retire easily.

She had been the nurse on shift when Marcos was exiled from the Philippines through the 1986 People Power Revolution and landed in Hawaii. A story she told with the reverence of someone who had witnessed a living myth, not a dictator. She adored the family, especially Madam. I didn't share her political fervor, but I loved her enough to let her have her version of history.

We sat in her living room trading stories, two generations of nurses with different memories of the Philippines, and I let silence do the bridging. Her persistence was its own migration — proof that where we land is never the full story of who we become.

Before I flew out, she tucked 50 U.S. dollars into my hand and said, *"Para hindi ka magutom."* Not much. But more than enough.

Hawaii: Freedom and Closure

Final stop: Hawaii. The beaches were postcards. The people, *aloha* embodied. I skydived again — my second time — and as I free-fell through summer air, I thought: *This is what freedom feels like.*

A trip like this doesn't just give you memories. It gives you mirrors. In every city, every mountaintop, masses and metro rides, I saw glimpses of the person I was becoming.

I didn't return with better grades or a heavier résumé. I came back with something rarer. A softened jaw. A slower heartbeat. And a conviction that the kind of lawyer I wanted to be wasn't the one who finished first, but the one who arrived whole.

I didn't just collect memories. I sent postcards. Reminders to my future self that wonder is worth pausing for.

A hundred days on the road, but never aimless. That summer wasn't a detour. It was a *return* — not to a destination — but to the version of me that paused, listened, and wrote it all down.

A reminder that fulfilment isn't found in the fast lane.
It's in the full breath before the next beginning.

And yet…

I thought I had traveled far. Across continents, through languages, within lifetimes folded into unfamiliar beds and border crossings.

But the longest journey was just beginning. The one with no passport stamps, no train timetables, no boarding gates. The one that asked me to sit still, sift through the noise, and meet myself without performance or plan.

And the hardest? It isn't geographic. It's internal — a reckoning beneath all the expectations, all the roles, all the scripts. Like migratory birds tracing invisible routes across continents, I moved not just for survival, but in response to a pull I couldn't yet name. They fly thousands of miles without maps, guided by something ancient and interior.

Migration isn't about where you land — but who you become in flight.

It's not just a change of geography, but of gravity — the slow recalibration of identity, courage, and becoming.

Bourdain had it right. You can cross oceans and still carry the same questions. What I carried into that trip — the pressure, the questions, the hunger to prove — came back quieter. Softer. Still there, but no longer in charge.

Because you don't always need a passport to cross into someone else's life. Sometimes, courage looks like sitting down, sharing a meal, and realizing you belong at the table.

—

I had wandered the world.
Now it was time to wonder inward.

Soul Notes

❖ What have you said yes to not to get ahead, but to come back to yourself?

❖ When were you last undistracted enough to truly hear yourself?

❖ What choice confused others but made you whole?

❖ What part of the world holds a version of you you're still becoming?

Chapter 11: The Journey to Oneself

"And you? When will you begin that long journey into yourself?"
— Rumi

The travel outward had stopped, *for now*. But the stillness I found
— that narrow breath between what was and what's next —
opened a different kind of path.

I once thought travel was measured in distance. Planes. Passports.
Packed bags. But the farthest journeys are often inward, crossing
not borders but beliefs.

Some journeys require documents. This one did not. There were
no guidebooks for the journey to oneself. Only time alone, and
truths that do not negotiate.

No currency except honesty.
No companions but memory, doubt, and grace.

I no longer needed a boarding pass. I needed the kind of courage
that appears only when the crowds disappear and the only witness
left is the person in the mirror.

Long before I set foot in a courtroom or swore an oath before the
New York Bar, I knew I wanted to be a lawyer. I could picture it
clearly. Standing in crisp black robes, wielding words like scalpel
and shield. Defending the underdog. Quoting obscure legal maxims
that would make a judge pause mid-coffee and say, *"Well, that was
clever."*

But in the Philippines, practicality often outranks poetry. Dreams
are folded neatly into utility, especially in families where ambition
must share space with necessity. Like many children of migrant
households, I was nudged, lovingly but firmly, toward nursing. It

was never cruel. Just cautious. A way of dreaming that made room for rent.

"It's stable."
"It's needed."
"It pays."

No one asked what my soul whispered late at night. No one asked if there might be a different road I was eager to take, one that would lead me closer to myself.

So, I became a nurse. Not because I failed to dream, but because I knew how to survive.

And to be fair, nursing gave me more than a paycheck. It gave me stamina. Perspective. An unshakeable spine. It taught me how to hold a hand when words fail. How to stay standing after twelve hours of compassion in overdrive, bureaucracy at your heels. It showed me what care looks like when it's exhausted but still shows up.

Still, that law dream did not disappear. It hibernated. Patient as hunger. Steady as something unresolved.

Some nights, after long shifts, I would scroll through social media and see former classmates in courtrooms or corporate offices. I would feel it then. Not bitterness. Just questions:
Did I play it too safe?
Was I called to something more, or just dreaming it?

What I did not understand yet was this.
The world doesn't always clap when you reach for more.

Immigrants like me are easiest to celebrate when we're serving. At the bedside, after hours, behind the scenes. When I wore scrubs, people called me *'selfless,' 'heroic,' 'noble.'* But when I spoke of law school or launching my own firm, the tone shifted. Not disapproval. Discomfort. As if I had stepped out of costume.

When you seek to lead, to argue, to bill, to own the table instead of just setting it, the celebration becomes silence.

I learned how unsettling it can be when you claim power others did not imagine for you. Law, I was told, was for people who belonged. Nursing was for people like me. Useful. Safe. Humble. It took me years to understand that *being needed isn't the same as being seen.*

Even my family worried. They wondered if I was making a fool of myself by wanting more. Not because they didn't believe in me, but because they knew how unforgiving the world can be to people who reach beyond their assigned place.

That's why pivoting felt radical. Not because ambition is rare, but because permission is.

I did not need permission. I needed proof. And I gave it to myself. In early mornings with legal textbooks. In late shifts fueled by caffeine and stubborn resolve. In the refusal to let the idea fade simply because it was inconvenient.

Years passed. Countries changed. I learned to speak softly in ICUs and clearly in visa interviews. But the legal calling persisted, steady and insistent. The longer I postponed it, the clearer it became that delay was no longer neutral. So, I said yes when staying safe began to feel lonelier than starting over. Not a cautious yes, but the terrifying, rent-is-due-and-I-am-still-studying kind.

Returning to school as a middle-aged adult is not for the faint of heart. Especially while working full time and packing Tupperware next to classmates who still lived with their parents. I survived on instant noodles, caffeine, and willpower.

I studied torts with a pulse oximeter beeping in the background. I prepped for finals in hospital break rooms, still in scrubs, smelling faintly of antiseptic and purpose. One time I highlighted the dosage instructions on a case summary out of habit. Old reflexes die slowly.

The loneliest part of chasing a dream no one expects of you is that no one clears the path. There were no cheering group chats. No blueprint. Just borrowed textbooks, online lectures, and the stubborn belief that I belonged, even when it did not look like it.

Law did not come easily. But when it clicked, it did so with precision. I could see structure where there had once been noise. I began to understand how words could do what even medicine sometimes could not. Restore dignity. Demand accountability. Make power answer for itself.

———

Finding your calling rarely arrives as clarity. It often comes dressed as chaos. The world offers detours, not red carpets.

The hardest part was never wanting more. It was accepting that stepping out of the script did not make me ungrateful. That I could want fully and still be worthy of the stage.

We live in a world obsessed with categories. Nurse or lawyer. Practical or passionate. Pick one. But my life never fit neatly into a single label. I would eventually accept that complexity is not a flaw. It is a fact.

I once believed that choosing nursing closed every other door. That the decision I made at fifteen was the entire story. My goal then was simple: *to serve the Filipino people.* I did not yet know I would be called to serve more. It would take oceans, night shifts, and a peaceful moment beside the Brisbane River to see it clearly. Nursing was not the end of the dream. It carried it until I was strong enough to choose it.

Sitting across from QUT, just outside the Brisbane Convention Centre after my Bachelor of Laws graduation in 2018, I watched the river move. It did not pause for ceremony. It did not rush. It simply followed its course. And in that motion, I understood something I had resisted for years. Progress does not always look like acceleration. Sometimes it looks like continuity.

Law was not something I had abandoned. It was something I postponed while learning how to survive. I had not failed the plan. I had followed it through a longer route, one shaped by necessity before choice.

This moment was about agency. About moving from being agreeable to being accountable. And that, too, is a form of service. One that begins when you stop asking whether you are allowed and start acting as if you are.

Passing the New York Bar years later would not be a climax. It would be confirmation. Proof that delay does not erase ambition. That persistence can carry an idea across borders, careers, and doubt without distorting its shape.

I am still walking this path toward alignment. Toward authorship.

I am a nurse. I am a lawyer. An immigrant who learned early how to be useful, and later how to be deliberate. I am no longer interested in proving that I belong. I am interested in deciding where I stand.

I'm not what the world drafted. I'm what I chose. A *rewrite* in italic.

—

Becoming an Australian solicitor and ICU nurse looked impressive on paper. But the real milestone was internal. And I knew there would be more.

Soon I'd learn what it meant to want more in a foreign language, with foreign laws, in a city that asked me to stand taller still. *Paris* was next. And with it, another mirror.

Soul Notes

❖ What part of yourself did you shrink to keep the peace and at what cost?

❖ Where have you chosen security over soul and why?

❖ If your life were rewritten today, what would no longer be negotiable?

Chapter 12: Pieces of Paris: Presence over Perfection

"If you are lucky enough to have lived in Paris as a young man, then wherever you go for the rest of your life it stays with you, for Paris is a moveable feast."
— Ernest Hemingway

Some people move to Paris for love. Others go for art, food, or the fantasy of walking along the Seine in a beret with a baguette tucked under one arm.

I came to Paris to study a master's in law, but what I found was wisdom which reshaped me slowly.

In 2020, I received a scholarship at the Sorbonne. It was the middle of a global pandemic. Borders were closing. Cities were locking down. People panic-buying toilet paper like it was Bitcoin. But when the best law school in continental Europe and one of the oldest universities in the world offers you a spot, you print your PCR test, pack your bags, and hope your face shield doesn't fog up at border control.

Paris greeted me not with romance, but with red tape. French bureaucracy makes Australia feel like a dinner party. I spent more time in *prefectures* than *pâtisseries*. But once I figured out the *métro*, the *boulangerie* down the street, and how to say *"Excusez-moi, je suis perdu"* convincingly, I started to feel, dare I say, local.

During the pandemic, Paris was a painting drained of color. Still arresting, but ghostly. *Paris in chiaroscuro: where memory and melancholy shared the same canvas.* Like an oil painting left in the rain — blurred edges, emotion intact. In Manila, I moved through crowds like a fish in a tide pool. In Paris, the emptiness startled me. There was room to stretch, but also to unravel.

The scent of croissants and cigarette smoke gave way to hand sanitizer and surgical masks. Cafés sat shuttered, their wicker chairs stacked like forgotten origami. The *métro* ran nearly empty, echoing with the coughs and the mechanical sigh of closing doors. Streets once alive with accordion buskers and camera shutters now echoed only the clipped footsteps of masked passersby, eyes lowered, pace brisk.

Even the Seine seemed to flow more cautiously, its banks fenced off like a wound. And yet, Parisians carried on. Baking bread, watering balcony plants, lighting candles in apartment windows as if to say: *We are still here. We are still Paris.*

Paris might have been in lock-down, but there was still the *savoir-faire*, the effortless elegance of doing things well without spectacle. The barista who could singlehandedly make you feel both underdressed and overcaffeinated with one raised eyebrow. The assortment of cheese beautifully lined up in a *fromagerie*. The elderly woman walking her dog in a Chanel coat — diplomat or just chic?

Eventually, I developed my own version. Navigating immigration forms, *métro* maps, and bakery etiquette with a half-smile and a folder of neatly labeled documents. That, *mon ami*, is survival *and* style.

Joie de vivre, quintessentially French phrase meaning *the joy of living*, showed up in unexpected places. Classmates dressed for Zoom lectures like it was Fashion Week. Strangers shared wine on the steps of the Panthéon. The unapologetic way Parisians enjoy their food, their time, and themselves. Not out of indulgence, but because they believe life should *feel*.

And for someone like me — an immigrant, an outsider — that kind of joy is subversive. To enjoy a pastry slowly, to linger over red wine, to inhabit joy in a city that doesn't fully see you. These are refusals. To find beauty anyway is to refuse erasure.

—

Some thresholds don't announce themselves. The Sorbonne was one of them. You only know you've crossed one when even your voice sounds different.

I had grown used to dusty classrooms in Davao, to plastic chairs and handwritten posters of the digestive system. But the Sorbonne? It was another universe entirely. It wasn't just a school. It was an arena — intellectual, emotional, unapologetically exacting.

The Sorbonne didn't whisper. It declared — in marble, in Latin, in centuries. Its walls held the weight of revolutions and dissertations, of poets who broke form and philosophers who broke faith. Light filtered through tall arched windows like benedictions. Dust floated in the air as if reluctant to settle, swirling in golden spirals over parquet floors worn thin by the heels of brilliance.

You didn't enter the Sorbonne. You entered into dialogue. With Voltaire, with Simone de Beauvoir, with ghosts who argued in French.

Outside, the courtyard pulsed with smoke and theory. Cigarette tips glowed like punctuation marks in debates about capitalism, Camus, and climate. Inside, the scent was a mix of old books, Chanel No. 5, and the slow burn of academic tension.

It was not a place that made you feel smart. It was a place that demanded you *become* smarter. Or at least quieter, more deliberate, more willing to disappear into a text and return changed.

The classes were intense. Studying there felt like trying to read poetry while holding your breath. It demanded rhythm, not just memorization. Respect, not just recall. Each doctrine felt like a debate between centuries. Each exam, a tightrope walk between tradition and reform.

—

At the *Cité Internationale Universitaire de Paris*, a student village built like a republic of dreams, I found breath again. In *Maison de l'Île-de-France*, I met, amongst others, Emily, Solène, and Simon from France, Yuna and Hong Zhu from China, Hestia from Hong Kong, Valentina from Colombia, and Ahmed from Mauritania — a country I hadn't even heard of until then. We traded stories, spices, and existential crises. One night, I hosted a Filipino dinner. My oxtail *bulalo* was met with reverent silence. The highest compliment.

The village felt like a rebellion against borders. Languages rustled like leaves through the tree-lined avenues. Cumin, curry, and croissants scented the air. Each hall was a cultural embassy: the red-brick British House, the serene *Maison du Japon*, the Moroccan pavilion tiled with gold.

On the lawns, students sunbathed, debated, or played music with Eurovision-level enthusiasm. Bach echoed through one wall, K-pop from the next. The cafeteria felt like the UN on a budget. There was *savoir-faire* in their posture, *joie de vivre* in their laughter, and *bienveillance* — kindness without suspicion — in how they made space for each other.

In a city that often made me feel like I had to prove my worth, this place reminded me I already belonged.

Paris taught me many things. Not all of them kindly.

Savoir-faire. Joie de vivre. Bienveillance.

Not just words — philosophies. And not gifts — tests.
Each one required effort, presence, and the courage to keep
becoming. Paris stripped away the illusion that merit guarantees
belonging, that beauty ensures kindness, that courage must be loud.
Presence, I learned, is power. Silence can be resistance. Style can be
survival.

And I also learned:

That love of the law is a universal language.

Paris gave me friends who lived and breathed law in different
dialects. Deborah and Gabriela from Brazil, Fjollë from Kosovo,
Paulina from Chile, Danae and Isidoros from Greece, Austin from
the United States, Tylor from Thailand, Alper from Turkey, Ola
from Poland, Angel from Mexico. We came from different
continents and stories, but at the Sorbonne, we spoke in one voice.
Curious, idealistic, and relentless in our belief that law could be
more than a system. It could be a language for change.

That to be is greater than to have. In French, *"Être est mieux qu'avoir."*

In Paris, I met people who weren't defined by status or salary, but
by conviction, curiosity, and how they moved through the world.
Their wealth was in books read, meals lingered over, questions
asked without apology. They didn't collect things; they cultivated
selves.

In learning how others live, I started seeing how I had been living
on autopilot. I unlearned some urgency, softened my sharpest

edges, and grew less obsessed with *'success'* — becoming more fluent in my own skin.

That perspective comes from the periphery.

When you see yourself through the eyes of another country, you begin to see what you couldn't from within your own. I saw my place — and power — in a way I never had before.

In its cobblestone streets and smoky cafés, I began to reconcile the many parts of myself. I walked where Sartre once brooded, where Hemingway once wrote, where Van Gogh once painted, where Curie once calculated, where revolutionaries once dared to ask, *"What if things were different?"*

Before Paris, I was ambition and apology. I knew my résumé. I didn't yet know my resonance. But Paris made me braver. Not in some grand, cinematic way, but in small, deliberate choices. Speaking up in class, sharing my story, standing taller in rooms where I once felt peripheral.

—

I thought I was beginning to find my place. But I hadn't yet learned what Paris would sound like when it didn't care to listen.

Like all icons, Paris has its shadows. For every moment of awe, there was also ache. One afternoon, in a blink, and a bit of naïveté, my backpack was *volé* — snatched. Gone were the essentials. Wallet, laptop, keys. And a tiny keychain — a gift from Yu-Meng, my friend in Brisbane. *"For good juju,"* she'd said.

Losing it wasn't just about sentimentality. It was like a small thread to home — and belief — had been severed. That keychain had traveled across borders with me. It reminded me that I wasn't alone, even when I was far from everything familiar. And now, even that was gone. Not by fate, but by force.

What was harder to lose was the illusion that beauty always comes with benevolence. At the *commissariat*, the police asked me to explain the details of the theft in fluent French. When I couldn't, their patience thinned. The message was clear: *Justice is often a native speaker. Fumble your verbs, and you risk forfeiting your rights. If you don't speak the language, your losses don't count.*

It wasn't just impatience. It was dismissal. Bureaucracy dressed in indifference. In Paris, language wasn't just communication. It was a border. And if you couldn't cross it, you didn't exist.

I hadn't come to Paris for romance, but somewhere along the way, I began to trust its polish. The city that offered elegance also enforced exclusion. The place that taught me law also revealed its blind spots.

It was my own version of *Paris Syndrome* — that heartbreak when reality doesn't fall short of the romance, but walks away with your laptop. The city of light, that had inspired poets and lovers and revolutions, now flickered with bureaucracy and indifference. It wasn't cinematic. It was cold.

And yet, Paris taught me to embrace the contradiction. That the city of Monet's lilies and Simone de Beauvoir's intellect could also be the city of pickpockets and paperwork. That even love, or a place you hoped to love, comes with its bruises.

Eventually, even bruises bloom into discernment. I came expecting a city. I found a mirror. And a question that lingers: *Can you still choose wonder, even when it doesn't choose you back?*

In the end, Paris promised *presence over perfection*. And the fullness of it — the tension, the tenderness, the occasional theft — was real. And real — raw, undeniable, and unrehearsed — is what I came for. And in that messy, mercurial way, it became part of me.

Hemingway was right. Not because Paris stays as you remember it, but because it keeps revealing who you've become.

I may not have come to Paris to channel Napoleon. But somewhere between the red tape, the lectures, and the slow courage it took to speak up in a second language, I found my posture. Not to conquer — but to remain.

Small men from tropical islands don't waltz into empires. We infiltrate them quietly, in well-ironed shirts, with just enough French to pass.

———

Next stop: *Deutschland: Land of Poets and Thinkers.*

Soul Notes

❖ What place in your life revealed the most about who you really are and not just who you were trying to be?

❖ When was the last time you said yes, not because you were ready, but because you were *done* waiting?

❖ Where did you once chase belonging and what did you find instead?

Chapter 13: Du bist stark. Du bist schön. Du schaffst das.

The European tour continued. Paris had been all soft light and self-revelation, a city that taught me how to feel again. Germany would teach me to hold it all together. If Paris was an inner awakening, Germany was the external reckoning. Where clarity wasn't poetic but practical. Where resilience didn't roar, but whispered, then welded. Where presence gave way to precision.

Paris had taught me how to soften. How to savor beauty, how to move with *savoir-faire*, how to live with a touch of *joie de vivre*, even in a city that didn't always see me. But soft living had its limits. Just as I began decoding French bureaucracy and semi-mastering the art of saying *Bonjour!* with conviction, life spun me in another direction — east.

Meine liebe Deutschland. Another country, another language, another set of rules to learn. But that's the thing about movement. You don't arrive with a map, just a mantra.

Frankfurt am Main, a city that looks like someone tried to mash up Wall Street, a fairy-tale village, and a Deutsche Bahn schedule that runs on time (mostly!), was my destination. It's where medieval timber-framed houses sit beside glass skyscrapers, where bankers hustle past *bratwurst* stalls, and where rules aren't suggestions but commandments.

I arrived at Frankfurt Hauptbahnhof in May 2023 after stints in Paris and Brussels, with my work contracts complete, and passport pages rapidly filling. I'd seen much of Europe by then. Some of it through train windows, some through sore feet, all through wide eyes.

Frankfurt is normally grey. But that day was *wunderbar. Guten Morgen, Sonnenschein,* indeed.

When I decided to move to Deutschland, I brushed up on my German not for a visa application or a holiday menu, but to live and work there. I wasn't aiming for Goethe-level fluency, but I knew I had to do more than order a coffee if I wanted to really belong. Somewhere in my notebook, I had scribbled *"meine liebe Deutschland"* thinking it was a sweet phrase. A poetic tribute. Only later did I learn that Deutschland is neuter, and the grammatically correct version was *mein liebes Deutschland.* A humbling reminder that even love letters need editing. Germany, it turned out, wasn't gendered, but it was exacting.

Learning to live in another language — to fumble through menus, conversations, and moments where your intelligence doesn't translate — is a specific kind of vulnerability.

I'd seen that up close with Yu-Meng, back when we were nurses together in Brisbane. Fresh from Taiwan, she didn't speak a word of English when she arrived in Australia. Back then, she used to go to Burger King and just point to *'Number 1'* (the lowest-effort order on the menu) because it felt safer than trying to speak. That was how she got by. Unobtrusively, resourcefully. She didn't complain. Slowly, bravely, she learned. Years later, she'd become one of the most respected nurses I worked with — confident, competent, and calmly fierce. Watching her taught me that fluency isn't just about words, but about *willingness.* The courage to stumble, to try again, to not let shame win. And now here I was, in Germany, channeling that same resilience. Mispronouncing *Krankenversicherung* (health insurance). Getting verbs in the wrong place. Hoping people would see the effort behind the accent.

Among the first phrases I committed to memory were simple but striking:
Du bist stark. Du bist schön. Du schaffst das.
You are strong. You are beautiful. You can do it.

At the time, I thought they were just handy phrases for encouragement. Something sweet to toss into small talk or a friendly text. I didn't yet realize those words would become a lifeline. A scaffold I'd cling to on the days when my confidence faltered and my ambition outpaced my energy.

How I got there was part miracle, part bureaucratic triathlon. I had secured a European Blue Card — the EU's answer to *"Do you have skills and not a criminal record? Willkommen!"* It's essentially a residence permit for highly skilled workers, assuming you tick the holy trinity: a recognized university degree, a valid job offer, and a salary high enough that you won't start a GoFundMe for rent. Check, check, check.

So, there I was, stepping into Germany with a suitcase full of legal notes, enough black sweaters to pass for a local, and a bar prep schedule so brutal I nearly burst into tears at a train station. Close call.

By day, I worked at a German law firm. By night, I studied for the New York Bar. And somewhere in between, I tried to pronounce *Rechtsanwaltskammer* without sounding like I was fighting off a sneeze and a stroke simultaneously.

Some nights, after twelve hours of parsing constitutional law, eyes barely focusing, I'd stare at my notes and wonder if I was delusional. Chasing too much, too far from home, in too many jurisdictions. And then that phrase would echo back to me, half-whisper, half-mantra:
Du bist stark. Du bist schön. Du schaffst das.

Not yet true. But something to grow into.

Frankfurt offered a strange vantage — gritty and polished, anonymous yet oddly intimate. The law firm plunged me into the precision-obsessed world of German and cross-border deals, arbitration tangles, and an operational efficiency that made my inner Scorpio purr. The colleagues? Razor-sharp and refreshingly blunt. But once you proved yourself — and brought baked goods — they let you in. (Tip: *Streuselkuchen* can do what a master's in law can't — open hearts.)

As the lone Filipino in the office, I figured I'd share a piece of home. I made *adobo* — rebranded as *'caramelized soy-braised pork with rice,'* because *'vinegar-forward'* didn't exactly ignite German appetites. It was a hit, if the scraped plates and second helpings were anything to go by. Turns out, the secret to cross-cultural diplomacy is garlic, bay leaves, and knowing when to translate flavor into familiarity.

Genau. That one magical German word that means *"exactly"*. And also, *"Yes, you get it," "We're aligned,"* and *'No further explanation needed."* A full-body nod in a single syllable.

But the heart of my Frankfurt chapter wasn't found in courtrooms or contracts. It lived in a windowed meeting room at the Frankfurt School of Finance & Management, in a club called Toastmasters. The same community I'd first stumbled into on the Gold Coast.

Toastmasters, as it turned out, was everywhere. A global community with local chapters. The same comforting rhythm of speeches, feedback, and spontaneous table topics, this time just delivered with a German punctuality and international flair. It was familiar and foreign all at once. Just like me.

In this Toastmasters, I met my people: Ivan, Nupur, Alex, Lisa, Christiane, Patience, Kim, Hana. A merry band of locals, expats, overachievers, and philosophical ramblers. We bonded over impromptu speeches, misused metaphors, cultural fumbles, and post-meeting *schnitzels* and *pilsners*. They were more than friends.

They were my anchor tribe in a city that was punctual but could be painfully isolating. They taught me that the most transformative friendships sometimes begin with two-minute speeches about the silliest of things, but leave you speaking your truth out loud. A little stronger, a little surer.

And while all that was unfolding — the laughs, the friendships, the growing fondness for *Riesling* — I was simultaneously grinding. Those awkward and vulnerable speeches under fluorescent lights weren't just practice runs for public speaking; they were rehearsals for real life. Toastmasters taught me to claim space, speak truth, and show up even when my voice trembled. That confidence bled into everything, including the journey toward the New York Bar.

The New York Bar as a Foreign-Trained Lawyer: A Saga

1. *Eligibility and Evaluation*: First, I had to prove that my Australian and French legal education met New York standards. That meant transcripts, course syllabi, formal letters, and what felt like the complete annotated autobiography of my academic life. The New York Board of Law Examiners (BOLE) reviewed it all with the warmth of a TSA agent before finally giving me the green light.

Then came the part no one warns you about. Not the paperwork, not the legal jargon, but the mental marathon of preparing for a test designed to break even the most caffeinated among us.

2. *Bar Prep*: I enrolled in a bar review course with BarMax and that took over my existence. U.S. constitutional law over *Apfelschorle* became my daily routine. I could quote Marbury v. Madison in my sleep. And often did.

It was during a particularly hard week, somewhere between civil procedure flashcards and an undercooked schnitzel, I came across the words again:
Du bist stark, du bist schön. Du schaffst das.

Germans aren't known for sentimentality. So, when moments of emotion come, they ring truer. And that day, I believed it. I was strong not because I didn't feel the weight, but because I carried it anyway. I was beautiful not for the way I looked, but for the way I kept showing up. I knew I could do it not because I was certain, but because I was willing to try.

3. *The Exam*: Two days. Six essays. Two case analyses. 200 multiple-choice questions. Enough legalese to make a Supreme Court clerk raise an eyebrow. Caffeine replaced blood. The Buffalo Convention Center in upstate New York was frigid enough to preserve organ donations, and the flickering overhead lights pulsed like they were rooting for my downfall.

I remember closing my eyes after Day 1 and feeling like my brain had been run through a shredder. I wasn't even sure if I'd written in English. Just verbs, statutes, and the distant sound of Marbury whispering, *"Good luck, kid."*

When it was over, I did what any spiritually confused bar candidate would do. I went to the American side of the Niagara Falls. The mist hit me like a baptism. I stood at the railing, damp, dazed, wondering if anyone had ever screamed *"Res ipsa loquitur!"* into the Horseshoe Falls just to let it all out. It was the most beautiful thing I'd seen in weeks. Mostly because it wasn't multiple choice.

4. *Multi-state Professional Responsibility Exam (MPRE)*: Because one exam wasn't enough, I had to prove I wouldn't rob

      clients or ghost them mid-litigation. Ethics, apparently, deserves its own ordeal.

5. *Character & Fitness*: A flurry of affidavits, fingerprints, moral character essays, and confirmation that I wasn't secretly a Bond villain. As if being a good person required a paper trail (maybe it does?).

6. *Swearing-In*: The final rite of passage. You raise your hand, swear the oath, and try not to ugly cry in front of a panel of judges who've seen it all, and probably failed half the applicants before you.

I passed.

I shared the news with my family and friends. They were all happy for me. For once, I let myself be proud. Without caveat, without apology.

I'm not entirely sure how.
Divine intervention? Leftover nursing grit? Toastmasters confidence? All three?

I didn't just earn the title *'New York Attorney.'* I earned the right to believe it. And in that triumph, I saw who I'd become. Someone who hadn't just survived the journey but grown into the words that once felt too big.

That moment felt like the world was giving me a high-five. I used to call myself legal *lasagna*: Filipino-born, Aussie-trained, Euro-seasoned. But after New York? I was *baklava*: intricately layered, spiced with grit, and sweetened by survival. Messy, but magnificent, and finally, whole.

—

I still don't know how I managed the law job, Toastmasters, and the Bar exam. All in under two years. I was living in a country I hadn't grown up in, hadn't trained in, whose language I could read but still fumbled in conversation. And somehow, I managed to pull off one of the most complicated professional transitions of my life. I marvel at that now. Maybe it was momentum. Or madness. Or it was just that German-influenced insistence.

For me, Frankfurt wasn't just a city. It didn't just test me; it tempered me. Like steel in fire. It didn't coddle. It clarified. It dissolved the doubt. It shaped my discipline. It reminded me that excellence doesn't require theatrics. Just persistence and prep.

Germany, despite its political influence and global financial impact, doesn't shout lessons. It whispers them until you listen. It's a country that surprises you with its softness after the structure, its warmth after the coolness. From Rothenburg ob der Tauber's postcard charm to Heidelberg's stillness and München's cultural pulse, Germany felt both ancient and futuristic, innovative but rooted. And the people? Discreet, yes. But strong. Creative. Loyal. Once they let you in, they stay.

To anyone who's ever felt overwhelmed by ambition or underprepared for their own potential:
Du bist stark. Du bist schön. Du schaffst das.

Say it. Believe it. Become it.

—

But even as I pushed forward, something else was starting to unravel behind the scenes. Something personal and far more difficult to navigate than law exams or language barriers. And no amount of discipline or drive could prepare me for what was coming.

I used to think those fighting words were only for the tough days at work. For when the legal codes got too dense or the loneliness too loud. But soon, I'd learn they weren't just fuel for ambition. They were a lifeline for grief.

And in the chapter that came next — the one I never wanted to write — those words would be the only ones I had left to hold.

In Paris, I learned how to become.
In Germany, I learned how to endure.
But I still hadn't learned how to *let go*.

That lesson would come next. Uninvited. Unforgettable.

Soul Notes

❖ What's the toughest test you've ever passed and what did it reveal about you?

❖ Where in the world did you most surprise yourself by showing up, speaking up, or simply staying?

❖ What truth or mantra carried you through your hardest season and do you still believe it?

❖ How has your definition of strength changed and what shaped that evolution?

Chapter 14: The Goodbye That Echoes

"I miss you more than I remember you."
— Ocean Vuong

Not everything you carry in life is a credential. Not everything earns applause or comes with letters after your name. Some of the heaviest things — like grief, love, or longing — never make it onto a résumé, but they shape you all the same.

In the middle of my time in Germany, a chapter marked by progress, bar prep, and professional growth, something inside me cracked. At home in the Philippines, Nanay got sick. The kind of news that doesn't land at once. It bounces off your logic, your plans, your time zones. And then sinks in like cold water.

Distance is a strange cruelty. You can be surrounded by sleek trams, five-bar reception, and flawless punctuality, but when someone you love is dying back home, you feel like you're on the moon.

Nanay's cancer began slowly. Like a fading signal. And then, without warning, accelerated.

I remember exactly where I was when the news came. In a library in Frankfurt, reviewing a non-disclosure agreement for a private equity firm while half-listening to a bar lecture. I was flanked by casebooks, caffeine, and the illusion that I could somehow hold everything together. Then came the group video call. While normally a chaos of emojis and reminders, this time it was a siren.

I answered. Their voices cracked — singularly and all at once — before the words could. *"Nanay is dying."*

And there she was. On screen. In a hospital bed. Her breath shallow, her eyes already drifting somewhere we couldn't follow. We held vigil through the screen, our faces pixelated by distance, our grief glitching through Wi-Fi.

And then, right there, between signal delays and stifled sobs, she took her last breath. We were with her, but some of us were not beside her.

There's no textbook for losing a parent. Just a slow ache of unfinished conversations and sudden flashbacks. Her scent on a sweater, her at the door as I left for college, her absence in places I never imagined without her.

Nanay passed with peace. As was her way. She didn't make demands of the world. A public elementary school teacher most of her life, she lived in service — to her students, her children, her community. Her love whispered. In warm plates of food. In uniforms perfectly ironed. In glances that said, *"Proud ko nimo ba"* without a single syllable spoken.

Even in her last days, she tried to protect me from the truth. *"Okay lang ko, Noy"* she'd tell me when I called her, her voice thin, her sentences slow. Even when her body was giving up, her love wasn't.

Nanay — Ilongga to the core — had a way of making even dying sound like a punchline. She wasn't theatrical, but her timing was lethal. Like Miriam Defensor-Santiago with fewer microphones and more sass. One evening, when she felt well enough to go out, we took her to a restaurant. She ordered the unhealthiest things on the menu — *sisig*, charred barbecue, a Coca-Cola — and when we looked at her in disbelief, she rolled her eyes and said, *"Mamatay naman ako, magkaon ta lami eh"* (*"Well, if I'm going to die anyway, can we at least eat something delicious?"*).

We laughed. Not because it was funny, but because it was *her*. Biting, matter-of-fact, and stubbornly alive, even as her body gave way. She never let illness steal her dignity. If anything, she made grief flinch first.

But not everything she said was cloaked in humor. Near the end, just before I returned to Germany after visiting her, she looked at me and said, *"Te Noy, mamiss mo ako?"* (*"Will you miss me?"*). It broke me in half. And those became the last words I ever heard her say in person.

I flew home. No hesitation. No bar exam, email, or German efficiency could hold me back. Chasing dreams and ticking life's shiny boxes suddenly felt irrelevant in the face of a silence I knew would never be filled.

I don't remember the airport. Only the ache and the silence that waited on the other side of customs — thick, heavy, unforgiving.

By the time I arrived in the Philippines, I faced the reality I'd long feared — the world without her in it. The room had her smell, her slippers, her rosary beads. Everything but her.

No final hug.

No whispered *"I love you"* exchanged bedside. Just fragments of memories like broken glass in my hands. The last video of her I recorded. Her handwritten letter when she visited me in Australia. The scent of her *malong* — the handwoven tube skirt from home.

And guilt. So much guilt. For being away. For not calling more. For choosing ambition over proximity. For chasing dreams in countries she'd never see. But the sharpest sting? Being a nurse who couldn't nurse her own mother in the end. Knowing exactly how to care — and still not being there to do it.

But I wasn't alone. My sisters — fierce, grounded, endlessly capable — had already taken the helm. They had been by Nanay's side in those final days, holding her hand, advocating for her care, managing the details I couldn't from afar.

The wake became a gathering of casseroles and candles, tears and *tsismis, mah jong* and memories. Even in mourning, my sisters made sure everyone was seen, heard, and fed. They welcomed strangers like family. They made space for sorrow and hospitality to coexist.

Giegie entertained the well-wishers with humorous and heart-warming stories (mostly about how she is the undisputed favorite) and fielded condolence calls like a diplomat. Nene and Hearty brewed coffee for guests as if grief could be softened with sugar. They didn't just manage the wake, they mothered our mourning. Nanay may have been gone, but my sisters carried her legacy and did what Filipino women have done for generations: turning grief into a communal act of remembering — sacred and slightly chaotic, like most family gatherings.

When I looked at my sisters, they had become our mother's hands, her voice, her presence in motion. And watching them, I realized maybe I hadn't failed her. Maybe love doesn't have to be local to be loyal. Maybe I was loving her — in my own way — from another time zone.

—

Not all grief echoes the same. When Tatay died, I grieved. But it was muted, almost abstract. His absence like an unfinished sentence. He was a man of his generation. One who measured love in sacks of rice, tuition receipts, and roofs that didn't leak. In his world, provision was affection, and presence meant staying the course — not sharing your heart.

But love without language leaves gaps. Authority often stood in for warmth. Discipline replaced dialogue. And sometimes, that traditionally paternal role calcified into emotional distance. He was unreachable in the ways that mattered most.

His absence, when he died, felt familiar. Like a continuation. Not a rupture. I didn't fall apart. I just… *paused.* What I mourned wasn't just the man, but the possibility of knowing him better.
And being known in return.

I've since learned that grief doesn't hinge on biology alone. It's shaped by the depth of presence someone held while they were alive. By whether their love felt lived, not just implied. And with Tatay, the emotional door was often shut before I ever learned how to knock.

With Nanay, it was different. Her love wasn't coded or withheld. It was spoken, served, and sewn into the dailiness of our lives. Her loss didn't just leave a space — it collapsed a sanctuary. When she died, I didn't just lose a parent. I became an orphan in the deepest sense. Emotionally, spiritually, viscerally.

Our relationship was unique. As I was the youngest of eight, by the time I was learning multiplication, most of my siblings had moved out. It was just the two of us often at home — well, us and the television that worked only when it felt like it. She had me at 42 — a bonus baby, as she liked to say — and I often joked that I arrived fashionably late to the party. But that lateness gave us something rare. Chill afternoons on the porch, just the two of us, where she'd hum old Visayan lullabies while I traced shapes in the dust. Because of our age gap, we were bonded in a way that felt outside time. I knew her not just as my mother, but as a woman — wise, weathered, and wonderfully human.

In 2017, when she visited me in Australia — it was her first time but you'd never know it — she glided through Sydney in tailored coats and patent shoes like she was running for office. We'd stroll along Circular Quay, her scarf tied just so, with the Opera House at her back and a full shopping bag in hand. She called the ferry *"our yacht"* and the Manly promenade her runway. People would stop us to compliment her. *"She's so elegant,"* they'd say. I'd beam and reply, *"She's always been that way."*

We'd sit at restaurants in Chinatown with menus she couldn't read, but she'd always order with confidence, be polite to everyone (which often annoyed me because if you didn't know her, you'd think she was patronizing), and tell me, *"Thank you, anak."* She posed beside the Harbour Bridge like she built it. I snapped photos, trying to preserve not just her presence, but her light. Her joy. Her ability to shower compliments even to strangers.

That year, we dressed up for special occasions and ordinary dinners alike. And in every photo, she had this soft, cheeky smile that said: *"Yes, I know I look good."*

We'd eat out, take photos, laugh. I tried to spoil her. She deserved it. But sometimes we'd fight because she'd always choose items for the *balikbayan box* instead of anything for herself. Lotion for a niece, biscuits for the neighbors, shoes for someone else's child. It frustrated me. I wanted her to choose herself — just this once. But that wasn't her way. Her instinct, always, was to give.

And it's funny that what once felt like injustice, I now carry with awe. Because it wasn't neglect. It was love — expansive and outward-facing. She didn't center herself because, in her eyes, love meant thinking of everyone else first. She parented the whole world. And I just happened to be lucky enough to call her mine.

Those days weren't grand, but they were gold. She didn't ask for much but she offered so much. Poise and playfulness I now see mirrored in how I carry myself. She showed me how to enjoy the world without entitlement. How to be warm. How to be kind.

—

As a young boy, I came across a horoscope which warned of tragedy early in Nanay's life. I don't remember the details, only the fear it planted. Long before I understood death, I was already bracing for hers. That was why I clung to her so tightly. I loved her as if time were already borrowing her back.

She outlived the prediction. Lived fully. Beautifully. But when she died, I was returned to that boyhood fear. This time, it had a name.

Nanay's death arrived like dusk. Slow. Golden. Impossible to hold. The kind of goodbye that doesn't collapse a house, but gently turns off the light, leaving the shape of everything you loved still visible in the dark.

Grief doesn't end. It echoes.
And an echo only exists because something once filled the room.

I carried her back with me to Germany. Back to bar prep. Back to work and ambition and the life that kept moving. The streets were the same. The textbooks unchanged. But I no longer moved through them untouched.

I carry her still. In how I lead. In how I listen. In the way I hold people when they are afraid. She never demanded praise. She taught by example. Calm. Kind. Unyielding when it mattered.

Her love shaped my leadership. Her poise shaped my professionalism. Her laughter shaped my humor. She wasn't just my mother. She was the architect of my strength. The whisper that steadied me before every exam. The soft, steady voice that always said: *"Kaya mo 'yan."*

If I have any superpower at all — emotional intelligence, grit, empathy, courage — she is its source.

She never stood in a spotlight. But she left something brighter behind. A love that learned how to echo. Across rooms. Across cities. Across languages.

So, when the world grows loud, I listen. Not for her voice exactly, but for the soft certainty it left behind.

I am still her son.
And she is still my compass.

—

I didn't want to admit it back then. Not while scrubbing in, charting vitals, or wrestling with a future that felt chosen for me. Nursing had never been my first dream. Law was. But Nanay saw something else. Something longer-range. She knew the world doesn't always reward passion first. Sometimes it rewards practicality.

"Pag-nursing na lang, Noy" (*"Just study nursing, Noy"*) she said once. *"Makatabang na ka, maka-abroad pa"* (*"You get to help others while being able to live abroad"*).

I rolled my eyes. I wanted to change the world, not wipe foreheads in foreign hospitals. Argue in court, not administer IVs. I thought she was steering me away from my dreams. I later realized she was pointing me toward them. Just taking the longer, safer road.

She was right all along.

Nursing opened the door. To the law. To the life I live now.
The detour wasn't a *'no'* to who I could become. It was a strategic
'yes' to getting me there safely.

Soul Notes

❖ Who taught you how to love and what version of love did they
leave behind?

❖ What wisdom are you still gathering from the people you've had
to let go?

❖ How has grief changed the way you show up for yourself and
for others?

Chapter 15: America Beckons: Return, Retry, Reclaim

Grief sharpens you if you let it. It clarifies.

After Nanay's passing, the ache didn't fade but something shifted. I stopped waiting for the perfect timing. I stopped negotiating with fear. And I began reaching for the one dream that had haunted me since nursing school: *America.*

Not the fantasy — but the unfinished business.
The test I failed. The visa that never came. The chapter that refused to close.

In 2008, I walked out of the NCLEX exam room devastated.
In 2025, I walked back in — older, braver, carrying every lesson Nanay left me with.

Seventeen years apart.
Same initials on the test paper.
Completely different man.

—

America doesn't always get the best press. It's loud, complicated, often on fire. Sometimes literally, sometimes legislatively. Between the gun violence, the political whiplash, and the healthcare system that charges $800 for sneezing in the ER, it's easy to develop a certain skepticism.

But most headlines won't tell you that once you get there — really get there — you'll see another America. The one with the Grand Canyon and the Yosemite that make you believe in God again. The one where strangers say *'Have a good one!'* and mean it. The one where your niece calls you her *'best friend'* before she's even met you in person. It's vast and maddening, yes. But it's also beautiful. And wildly, achingly full of promise.

And that promise — that slightly dented but still dazzling American Dream — is what called to me.

I didn't go chasing the American Dream for glory or Twitter followers.

I followed it because I wanted to be near my sister Nora and her family — for birthdays, soccer games, school concerts, and Costco runs that felt like full-blown expeditions. Because FaceTime was no longer enough. I wanted to be there — not digitally, but humanly. Fully.

That was the emotional driver.

The professional one? Oh, that was pure chaos and symmetry. I wanted to complete the most absurd Venn diagram of qualifications known to man: nurse in Australia, lawyer in Australia, nurse in America, lawyer in America. A bureaucratic haiku of legitimacy. A paper trail that would make a USCIS officer weep from joy (or confusion).

But no epic begins without its detour.

Cue the NCLEX.

Ah yes. The nursing licensure exam designed to test your clinical competence and your emotional stability. Often simultaneously. A pop quiz wrapped in existential dread, tied with a bow of sleep deprivation. The test is simple: *Can you keep a straight face while being asked how to titrate dopamine while your soul quietly disassociates?*

The first time I took the NCLEX, I didn't tell many people. Just my family. I was 21, full of ambition, and utterly unprepared. I walked out of that exam center in Makati, a city in Metro Manila, already rehearsing how to explain my failure. I stared at the screen for a full minute, the low hum of the testing room suddenly louder than my thoughts, before I closed it and never opened it again. I didn't cry. I didn't rage. I just folded the moment up like a mistake you pretend never happened.

I shelved that dream, told myself it wasn't meant to be, and poured everything into what came next — ICU work, law, new countries, new qualifications. Life, as it often does, got louder. And yet, somewhere in the static, a small voice refused to go quiet. Seventeen years later, I heard it clearly again.

Seventeen years. That's how long it took me to circle back to the NCLEX. In those years, I had crossed oceans, worn white coats and black robes, grieved losses, built businesses, and survived systems that weren't built for people like me. But the unfinished business of that exam haunted me — not because I needed another credential, but because it felt like a door I had once knocked on, then walked away from.

When I finally decided to retake it, I didn't announce it. I studied in silence. Early mornings before shifts, evenings after client calls, weekends when my brain was fried from legal research. I pulled out my old nursing notes like sacred scrolls. Some still held my 21-year-old handwriting — hopeful, slightly frantic, heartbreaking. I added sticky notes over the old ones, like a conversation across time.

I memorized lab values while stirring pasta, whispered mnemonics to myself in the shower, and studied between shifts like it was a secret mission. I told no one — not out of shame, but because this time, it wasn't about proving anything to the world. It was about finishing something I had started almost two decades ago.

When the result came in, I didn't scream. I didn't cry. I just smiled
— wide, grateful, stunned.

I passed.

I walked outside, and for the first time in weeks, noticed how clear
the sky was. It was a moment of deep, anchored calm. Like
something inside me had finally unclenched.

At 38, passing the NCLEX didn't launch a career. It closed a loop.
It healed something. It reminded me that we don't always get
second chances, but when we do, we can meet them with steadier
hands and a softer heart.

Succeeding after a failure also taught me that sometimes the
bravest thing you can do is return to the place where you once
failed. To carry yourself across the threshold you weren't ready for
back then.

Seventeen years ago, I failed that test and assumed the dream
ended. But dreams don't die. They wait until you're steady enough
to return without desperation. Back then, I wanted America to save
me. This time, I wanted to meet it on my own terms.

America, in many ways, had always been the backdrop of my
ambition. But now, it wasn't just an idea. It was a destination. One
I could finally walk toward without a shadow of unfinished
business at my feet.

Passing the NCLEX seventeen years later wasn't a triumph over
time. It was a reunion with an earlier version of myself who had
dared to dream big before he knew what failure cost. And in that
reunion, something powerful happened. I didn't just reclaim a goal;
I reclaimed my own timeline.

America didn't just beckon. It met me where I was, older, steadier, and finally *ready*.

And that's the thing about America. The policies will change. The news will stay dramatic. But dreams? They're borderless. They endure administrations, inflation, visa queues, and even your own self-doubt.

Dreams don't ask for perfect timing. They ask for movement. They ask for patience. They ask for snacks. (Always pack snacks.)

So yes — move, even with fear in your pocket and past failures whispering in your ear. Move, even if the world tells you you're too late. Move, because positivity isn't naïveté. It's strategy. It's how you survive long enough to see the plot twist.

As Samuel Beckett said: *"Ever tried. Ever failed. No matter. Try again. Fail again. Fail better."*

I learned to fail tenderly. And then to move forward anyway.

—

The life events up to this point all became the spine of my courage. But they weren't just milestones; they were acts of defiance. A thousand moments of persistence, of showing up, of choosing movement when stillness felt safer. It was a courage forged not in grand gestures, but in resilience, grit, and emotional fluency.

But courage, while essential, isn't the whole story.

Courage gets you through the door. *Becoming* is what happens once you're inside.

Soul Notes

❖ What failure have you left gathering dust and is it time to dust off the dream, too?

❖ What version of yourself did you bury and what would it take to resurrect them?

❖ If the chaos never calms, will you keep waiting or start anyway?

❖ Where in your life have you mistaken caution for wisdom?

PART III:
BECOMING

Chapter 16: Sydney, Scrubs, and Statutes

Becoming sometimes reveals itself on familiar ground.

I did not come back to Australia to begin again. I came back to claim what had already been forming.

Ten years after first arriving as an immigrant, I returned in late 2024 with the clarity that comes when life stopped fragmenting. I arrived carrying more than European memories and expired *métro* cards. I arrived to integrate what had once been kept apart. The plane window was smeared with rain, the low vibration of the engine settling into my bones. I caught my reflection and met the stranger I was finally ready to know.

I didn't always know Sydney would be home. I had visited before and was charmed by the postcard clichés: the glowing Opera House, the harbor like spilled sapphire, the cinematic rhythm of ferries cutting through the water. But visiting a city is a fling. Living in one is a marriage. Flings are fireworks. Marriages are the slow burn of morning coffee in the same chipped cup.

When I first landed in Queensland, I tried. I nodded through small talk that overstayed its welcome. I was grateful — for the job, the safety, the sunshine. But I couldn't shake the feeling I was wearing someone else's shoes. They fit, technically. But they weren't mine.

So, I moved.

Sydney met me not with fanfare, but with familiarity, as if it had been waiting. Somewhere between my first bus ride, the driver humming 80s ballads, and my fourth overpriced flat white, I knew. This was the Australia I had been craving. A city stitched together by languages, stories, and spice racks from five continents.

The scent of *laksa* curled out of Chinatown alleys, mixing with the warm clatter of outdoor tables in Haymarket, where strangers ate shoulder to shoulder beneath buzzing red lanterns and menus laminated into permanence. The summer air was sticky with eucalyptus and ambition. It wasn't one moment but the layering of it all, like spices folded into broth until they became inseparable.

Walking along Pitt Street near Darling Harbour, I looked around and saw Chinese students laughing over *boba*, Indian families heading to temple, Irish nurses finishing a night shift, Latinx teenagers being gloriously loud in a food court. Everyone was from somewhere. But here, we all belonged. No one stared, whispered, or asked why we were here. For the first time in years, my difference dissolved instead of defining me.

This city was real. This was mine. This was home.

And this time, I wasn't passing through. As an Australian citizen, I could leave, yes. But I could always come back. That kind of security mattered.

But Sydney didn't just offer belonging. It offered convergence, a folding in of the many selves I'd long kept compartmentalized.

To maintain my nursing registration with the AHPRA after not practicing nursing for a few years, I returned to hospital life. This also meant I could get my EB-3 immigrant visa application underway, a U.S. program for skilled workers like nurses and a pathway to live and work in the United States permanently. A priority date appeared on my file, now the wait began.

Back in scrubs, I found myself in the intensity of a Cancer Care ICU. Of all the wards I could've landed in, it was one devoted to cancer as if, somehow, this was my way of honoring Nanay. Her story, her suffering, her strength — now stitched into the seams of my scrubs. But this time, the paperwork wasn't for a client. It was for me. I wasn't just preparing case files — I was the case file.

The U.S. immigration system wasn't built for warmth. It was built to test how long a person can hold on to hope before it breaks into resignation. Navigating it was opening Pandora's box, except instead of mythical curses, it was paperwork, shifting timelines, and decisions that could change a life because of a single misplaced date. And yet, just like the myth, there was always one thing left at the bottom: *hope*.

Being back in nursing was heavy on the back, heavier on the soul. Grief sits bedside. Sons lose fathers, women pray with cracked voices, breaths come slow and final. The body aches; the spirit bends. But still, somehow, it grounds me. It tethers all my abstract ambitions to something real, raw, and sacred.

And then, after the hospital shift, the other me clocked in. I changed out of my scrubs, folded them over the back of a chair, and opened my laptop while the kettle came to a boil. While the ICU buzzed with beeping monitors and soft cries, I was building something else. A response to a life lived across borders.

I watched migrants move through Sydney carrying more than suitcases. They carried timelines from multiple countries, credentials that expired in one system while still pending in another, and decisions that could not be made in isolation. Too often, they lost time, money, and hope not because they lacked ability, but because no single system could hold the full picture of their lives.

I knew that feeling intimately. I was living it.

ONOR Immigration Law, registered in New York, and ONOR Advisory, an Australian company, were born for people who navigate oceans of red tape across borders, time zones, and legal cultures. Built from my passports and professions as a bridge for people caught between countries, languages, identities, and aspirations.

When it came time to name the firm, I chose my family name, *Onor.* Not as branding, but as a stake in the ground. There would be nowhere to hide. Every decision, every error, every success would carry my name. A risk. Failure would be personal. But so would accountability. ONOR was not a promise of perfection, only of care. Of standing close enough to where I came from that my work could be judged honestly.

Opening the businesses was not glamorous. It was spreadsheets and sweat. Early mornings with immigration memos, late nights answering call bells. Toggling between latex gloves and legal briefs. Adrenaline and affidavits. Scrubs and statutes.

And yet, it felt seamless. Two rooms in the same house. Two kinds of emergencies. One singular heart.

It wasn't magic, it felt close.

It was the same *empathy with an edge* — the kind I'd honed long before ONOR had a name.

Nowadays, ONOR Immigration Law serves clients who need expert navigation of the U.S. system, often before their first plane ticket is even booked. ONOR Advisory runs the operations and manages the systems, compliance, and regional strategy.

It's a marriage of what I know and what I love — advocacy, precision, care. The discipline demanded in hospital bedsides grounded my approach to immigration law. One world taught me how to hold space for suffering. The other, how to build bridges through bureaucracy. Together, they made meaning.

Sydney, with all its layered light and unapologetic pace, made space for both. Funny how long it takes to arrive at a place you've already unpacked in.

For a while, I thought Europe was a detour. A beautiful, chaotic misstep. But it wasn't. It was the confusion before the clarity. The unraveling before the rebuild. If I hadn't wandered, I wouldn't have known what it felt like to arrive.

And arriving here meant something radical. I was finally ready to lead and build a legacy. Not someday. *Now*. Here. In this humming, multicultural, caffeinated city where people hustle with heart in equal measure.

So yes, I came to Australia for a job. But what I found was a city that let me wear all my uniforms at once. A place that did not force a choice between precision and empathy, between nurse and lawyer, between ambition and home. Sydney did not ask me to erase my past. It asked me to bring it to the table. I did not pivot. I integrated.

Scrubs, statutes, and the stories in between — they all belong here.

—

In a world rushing forward, Sydney taught me the value of staying put. Of reading not just books, but places, people, and my own unfolding. To return to the slow, sacred act of paying attention. To treat my life — all of it — as literature worth lingering on.

And that's what Sydney returned to me most of all. A place to build and the capacity to pay attention again. To the clink of teaspoons in Chinatown cafés. To the shuffle of nurses trading night shift stories on King Street in Newtown. To the stillness tucked between sirens.

To *read* the world — and myself — more slowly.

Soul Notes

❖ When was the last time you didn't just fit in but belonged?

❖ Which parts of yourself deserve to sit at the same table, instead of being kept in separate rooms?

❖ What so-called detour turned out to be your actual map?

❖ What if the life you're building already *is* the dream and not the compromise?

Chapter 17: The Lost Art of Reading

"A reader lives a thousand lives before he dies. The man who never reads lives only one."
— George R.R. Martin

After building something that finally felt true, I did not want to rush forward. I wanted to stay still long enough to understand what had changed. To sit with the scrubs, the statutes, the city that had learned my name. When motion paused, I returned to the practice that had always oriented me: *Reading.*

Reading was never an escape. It was how I learned to stand upright in unfamiliar worlds.

Before visas, before borders, before credentials, there were books. In Gubatan, I would stretch out under a mango tree with a paperback balanced on my chest, bare feet brushing dry soil. Nanay would call for help with the laundry, and I would pretend not to hear, too deep inside borrowed lives. Pirate queens. Romantic heroines. Encyclopedias missing entire volumes. Books were my first geography lesson. My first proof that life could be larger than the perimeter I had inherited.

I remember reading *Harry Potter* for the first time, long before it became cultural shorthand. I could not stop turning the pages. I was startled by how a boy from rural Philippines could recognize himself in a wizard raised in a cupboard under the stairs in Surrey. The magic was not the spells. It was persistence, loyalty, and the search for belonging in places that did not initially want you. It taught me something I would return to:
Beginnings do not determine becomings.

When the world around me felt misaligned, books became my translators. They gave language to emotions I could not yet name.

My heroes were not invincible. They were confused, stubborn, afraid. They survived not by certainty, but by staying present long enough to grow.

The Fault in Our Stars taught me that a short life can still be full. That love does not shrink just because time does. Death does not erase meaning. It sharpens it.

The Catcher in the Rye made uncertainty feel livable. Holden Caulfield's refusal to perform adulthood on command reframed adolescence for me, not as a delay, but as a furnace. Confusion was not weakness. It was formation.

Books also shaped my relationship to country. *Noli Me Tangere* did not simply teach me history. It taught me moral courage. Rizal showed me that writing could confront power without surrendering dignity, that words could bruise empires through clarity alone. Patriotism, I learned, was not obedience. It was responsibility.

As my life expanded, the settings changed. The mango tree became a bed with clean sheets and too many pillows. The books changed too. Novels gave way to legal texts, essays on ethics, long arguments that demanded patience. But the ritual endured.

After days that leave me threadbare, I do not crave distraction. I crave depth. I want to sit inside a question long enough to understand it. Stories hold you when your own thoughts feel crowded. And sometimes, they return you to yourself.

There was a moment I did not expect reading to matter so much. I was listening to a client tell their story, fragmented, emotional, afraid of being misunderstood. Earlier versions of me might have rushed to solutions. But reading had trained me otherwise. To listen for subtext. To notice silence. To hold competing truths without collapsing them. That is when I understood that reading had not just shaped who I was. It had shaped how I judged, how I listened, how I carried responsibility.

Lord of the Flies unsettled me because it told the truth. Civilization is fragile. Order is learned. Survival does not automatically produce virtue. But it does not have to erase it either.

The Hunger Games reframed survival as defiance. Katniss, a girl from the margins, reminded me that systems feel permanent only until someone refuses their terms.

And yet, somewhere along the way, we misplaced the conditions that make reading possible.

We lost the *pause*. The patience required for a long argument. The humility demanded by nuance. The willingness to sit with discomfort without reaching for distraction. Our attention fractured. Empathy thinned. Silence became suspect. We learned to skim instead of stay.

I did not notice the loss immediately. But between algorithmic chatter, performative conversations, and the pressure to react, I began to miss the version of myself who trusted slowness. The one who believed depth was not indulgence, but discipline.

So, I returned to the page. Some books met me like companions who knew when to speak and when to listen. *Shantaram* carried me across continents and moral terrain, asking hard questions about loyalty, redemption, and the cost of belonging.

Sapiens unsettled my certainty by reminding me that nations, money, and rights are shared stories. Temporary agreements we behave as if eternal. In cosmic time, we are brief. That brevity makes meaning more urgent, not less.

Michelle Obama's *Becoming* dismantled the myth that legitimacy requires conformity. Her steadiness made room for my own.

Ocean Vuong's *On Earth We're Briefly Gorgeous* taught me that fractured language can still hold truth. It gave grief a grammar.

Every book became a mirror. I was not just absorbing ideas. I was recognizing myself, my hunger, my fear, my capacity for growth. Between lines, I found reckoning.

I reread *The Alchemist* as an adult. Less romantic. More attentive. What once felt like destiny now read as responsibility. The lesson remained. You may have to leave home to learn what was always yours.

Books never asked for my credentials. They did not care about my accent or passport. For someone born at the margins, reading was not leisure. It was preparation. A way to think clearly, speak precisely, and enter rooms already fluent in complexity.

Reading trained my attention. It taught me how to listen before speaking. How to hold contradiction without needing to resolve it prematurely.

Books taught me that villains are often wounded, heroes incomplete, and truth inconvenient. That transformation rarely arrives through force. It emerges through presence.
If it has been a while since a sentence stopped you, find one. Let it unsettle you. Let it slow you down.

Because in a culture addicted to noise, reading is resistance. It restores imagination, patience, and interior life. Pause not for the scroll, but for the sentence that asks something of you. Sometimes what you are searching for is not in the next update, but in the line you almost skipped.

This is the miracle. Through words written by strangers, we find ourselves reflected. Across centuries and cultures, connection persists.

What we need is not just more books, but a recovery of attention. Readers do not simply consume ideas. They cultivate judgment. And judgment is how we remain human.

—

For me, the next chapter would not be bound in paperback. It would unfold across countries and choices, written in two tongues, mine and my mother's. Like the books that shaped me, it would begin gently, asking for attention before offering meaning, and end with belonging.

Books taught me how to connect across centuries, how to listen to voices shaped by different worlds and still recognize myself in them. Travel would later teach me how to connect across cultures, with nothing but a smile, a misstep, and the willingness to stay present. Reading trained me for stories written in ink. Travel handed me those written in gestures, glances, and broken translations. Different grammars, same demand. Attention. Humility. Patience.

Both insist on the same truth: *Meaning survives distance.*

Soul Notes

❖ What book trained you to listen more carefully to the world?

❖ Which story taught you how to hold complexity without fear?

❖ If your bookshelf were a map, where would it say you are heading next?

Chapter 18: Lost in Translation, Found in Connection

"Borders are scratched across the hearts of men, by strangers with a calm, judicial pen."
— Pavel Antokolsky

Nanay spoke in a cadence that did not always match mine. Our sentences bent in different directions, our grammar rarely aligned, yet we understood each other anyway.

Understanding came through shared silence. Through gestures that required no explanation. Through food passed across the table before hunger ever had to be named. Long before I crossed borders, I learned that *comprehension does not always arrive dressed as language.*

Years later, travel would return that lesson to me, more complicated but no less true. Over time, I learned that connection rarely depends on fluency or shared history.

Books taught me how to connect across centuries. They gave me timelines and reference points, allowing me to walk with pharaohs, argue with philosophers, and survive imagined futures. Reading trained my mind to stretch across time.

Travel demanded something else. It asked me to stretch across people. It required no flawless grammar or polished itineraries, only a smile, a stumble, and the willingness to be human in unfamiliar places.

I do not take that privilege lightly. I am deeply grateful for a life that allowed me to move between worlds, to learn through motion, to be shaped by cities and strangers and shared meals. Every border crossed carried a lesson. I learned that growth does not always arrive through achievement, but often through exposure and discomfort. Not everyone gets to live this way. I did. And I carry that gratitude with me.

—

We live in a time when the world feels louder and more brittle than it once did. Wars unfold across screens in real time. Borders harden. Language sharpens. Everyone speaks at once, convinced of their own certainty, and yet misunderstanding has never felt so widespread. What fractures us now is not a lack of information, but a loss of attention. We know more than ever and understand each other less.

Travel stripped away any temptation to romanticize that truth. Not all crossings are equal. Some of us move through airports with ease, while others clutch documents like proof of worth, navigating systems never designed to welcome them. I learned to smile through security lines built on discreet suspicion, where speaking English is still not enough and understanding is too often optional.

For years, I chased credentials instead of conversations. I believed that if I followed every rule, prepared thoroughly, and presented myself correctly, I would be understood. But in visa queues and borrowed cities, I learned something humbling. You can speak the language and still be misunderstood. You can follow the rules and still be rejected. You can arrive fully documented and still feel invisible. It slowly dawned on me that many of the spaces I entered were never built with me in mind. I was not simply learning how to belong. I was translating myself into acceptability.

And yet, connection kept finding me anyway.

In a visa queue in Frankfurt, I stood clutching documents as my heart thudded louder with every shuffle forward. The woman beside me, also brown and visibly exhausted, handed me a pen without a word. There was no backstory, no conversation, just a small, unremarkable act of kindness that landed precisely because it was unremarkable.

A similar kindness met me in Istanbul. I was short a few *lira* while trying to board a ferry, already tired from navigating a city that felt louder and faster than my confidence allowed. Martim, a Portuguese student standing nearby, noticed and covered the fare. He never asked my name. He simply helped, as though my difficulty were ordinary and my dignity intact.

In Scandinavia, I learned that rest could be ceremonial. Coffee poured. Pastries shared. Candles on tables. Wool sweaters. Silence that did not need filling. *Fika* and *hygge* carried the same wisdom in different accents: that presence matters, that pauses deserve protection, that connection does not require urgency.

Human connection does not always require history. Sometimes it requires only empathy, and often a shared ache. Across countries and currencies, I encountered the same desires: to feel safe, to be fed, to laugh, to belong. No matter the time zone or exchange rate, that longing proved universal.

—

Before travel, I believed identity was fixed, inherited, defined by birthplace and accent. Over time, I learned otherwise.

In New Zealand alpine huts, strangers became companions by nightfall. We were no longer job titles or hometowns. Just people with blisters, half-eaten trail mix, and shared fatigue. Endurance stripped us down to something simpler.

Travel taught me that language is unreliable, but connection, when it happens, is remarkably steady. You miss trains. Point at menus you cannot read. Share rooms with strangers who snore like freight trains. Disorientation loosens assumptions. Judgment softens. Certainty gives way to curiosity.

In Krakow, I prayed beside strangers at World Youth Day, surrounded by Brazilians, Italians, and Filipinos singing the same hymn in different tongues. We did not understand each other's words, but the shared identity was unmistakable. Faith filled the gaps language left open.

Still, travel refused to remain poetic without consequence. Borders may be imagined, but their effects are not. Passports function as permission slips, determining who is waved through and who is held back. Immigration is not a meritocracy but a hierarchy, one in which power speaks the native tongue and privilege wears a particular accent.

In Rome, while attempting to register a phone number, a man muttered, *"Foreigners,"* under his breath. I pretended not to hear. The woman behind him did not. Without performance or pause, she said, *"We were all foreigners once,"* then smiled at me briefly. The moment passed quickly, but it stayed.

Difference itself is not the problem. Disconnection is. We live in a world that rewards certainty and punishes nuance, where outrage trends and complexity is inconvenient. Travel interrupts that impulse. When you share bread with someone who does not pray like you, or laugh beside someone whose politics oppose yours, curiosity replaces certainty.

Travel will not fix the world. But it expands the room inside you, increasing your capacity to hold complexity without rushing to flatten it.

—

Standing beneath the Acropolis, with the sun pressing against ancient marble and grit in the air, I felt small but not diminished, like a comma in a sentence that began millennia before me. My backpack was heavy with paperwork. My chest was heavier with homesickness. Around me, strangers drifted past in borrowed awe. I have seen the landmarks. But it is never the monuments I remember most. It is the people.

In Brazil, a host brought me to a *favela* where he ran a dance program for children. They smiled at me as though I were a cousin who had wandered home from somewhere shinier. In Fiordland, I shared tea with Sophia, a hiker from Hong Kong, our conversation sparse but our silence full. In Granada, Alejandro led me through the Alhambra not to impress, but to share. I left with fewer photos than expected, but with a clearer sense of how generosity can look like invitation.

The real souvenirs are not objects. They are the human moments that outlast geography. Landmarks impress. People imprint. Years later, I cannot always recall the order of cities. But I can still picture the smiles, the pauses, the invitations. That is what stays.

—

Some of the bravest journeys I have taken did not involve crossing oceans. The first time I spoke at Toastmasters in Frankfurt, my opening joke fell flat. I kept going anyway. When they clapped, it was not polite applause. It was something warmer, earned through persistence rather than polish. That night, I realized I did not have to arrive perfect to belong. I just had to stay.

One afternoon in Sydney, leaving the gym with headphones in and my schedule full, I noticed an older woman struggling with two suitcases near the stairs. I almost walked past. Then something tugged. I offered help. She accepted.

She was visiting from Canberra. Her son was having heart surgery. She spoke with a calm that felt earned rather than rehearsed. As we walked, we found small overlaps. She edited books. I wrote one. Her son was a lawyer. So was I. She had lived in Belgium. I had too. She spoke French. I could manage *oui*.

She was eighty, though you would not have guessed it. Her face carried peace. When we parted, I realized I had been handed more than a moment of connection. I had been shown a possible future. Someone who carries tenderness.

Travel, I came to understand, is not measured in miles but in mindset.

—

Migration, however, is travel that allows you to stay changed. Travel lets you pass through. Migration asks you to plant roots in unfamiliar soil without guarantees. Each time I migrated, I did not merely enter a new country. I entered a new version of myself, one forced to translate warmth into paperwork, memory into proof, belonging into addresses and forms.

Travel has souvenirs. Migration has systems. Travel leaves you with photos. Migration leaves you with files, queues, and waiting rooms.

Migration is quieter than travel, less postcard and more patience. A bank account opened. A rental contract signed. The tax return filed. Something bureaucratic that feels unglamorous but real. But it offers something deeper. A belonging built through repetition. A coffee shop that knows your order. A friend who checks in when you are sick. A place that eventually feels chosen rather than endured.

I used to think home was something you found. Now I know it is something you build, and in building it, you become. Being lost in translation does not mean failure. It is the place where connection begins

That was Nanay's lesson all along. She did not ask to be understood. She fed me first. She sat beside me. She stayed.

—

If *100 Days of Summer* was about learning how to rest, this chapter is about learning how to reach. Not to conquer or collect, but to connect. The next chapter will not come with stamps or souvenirs. It will come with sacrifice, because every dream carries a cost, and the noblest ones often demand payment in silence.

The invitation remains. To listen longer than comfort allows. To stay present when explanation fails. To offer something small before it is asked for.

Empathy still grows the same way it always has. Across a table. In shared silence. With food passed hand to hand.

Soul Notes

❖ When did you last allow yourself to be the beginner?

❖ What connection surprised you not because it made sense, but because it made you feel seen?

❖ Where in your life might understanding begin without words?

Chapter 19: The Quiet Cost of Dreams

In the last chapter, I wrote about how travel taught me to connect. With strangers. Across tables. In places like Rio's *favelas* or New Zealand's alpine huts. Connection nourishes the soul. But it does not stretch the budget. It does not buy time off. It does not cover exam fees or rent when the exchange rate turns against you. Even connection costs something.

And when you chase a dream without a financial safety net, that cost arrives silently. Especially when you carry a Filipino surname. Especially when failure is not an option you are allowed to consider.

Before the celebrations came the sacrifices. Long before the diplomas, titles, or visas, there were days spent working when I wanted to rest. Nights studying when I wanted to sleep. Years of saying *'not yet'* without knowing whether the dream would ever pay me back.

There is a popular image of hustle culture. Flashy. Motivational. Triumphant. But hustle is not glamorous. It looks like declining dinners with friends. Exhaustion that no weekend can repair. Missing birthdays and holidays because you picked up another shift. Choosing stamina over joy.

I grew up where budgeting was not a skill. It was survival. We did not just stretch pesos. We stretched patience. We watered down shampoo. Added more water than rice. Made decisions based not on desire, but on delay. What could wait. What must wait. What would never make the list.

So, when I became an Overseas Filipino Worker, the financial tightrope did not disappear. It only got longer. Abroad, I was not just adapting to a new country. I was navigating systems that applauded my grit without questioning why it was required. I was praised for stretching, not because it was noble, but because the structure was never built to catch me if I fell.

Working overseas often means living two parallel lives. One where you work. One where your heart lives.

Your paycheck arrives in one currency. The emotional toll is charged in another. You measure your worth not by what you keep, but by what you send. Tuition. Hospital bills. Birthdays marked through bank transfers. You earn in silence and give with urgency.

We are taught our value is in what we give.

So, we send remittances instead of postcards. We show up through Western Union, not holidays. We carry pride in silence and love in boxes. There is beauty in that. And sometimes, suffocation.

There is an intimacy in tracking exchange rates like the stock market. One day your dollar is king. The next, you are asking your sibling to wait a week before withdrawing. I know remittance fees better than I know my own blood pressure. I know the difference between good shampoo and the one that smells like compromise and aloe vera from a convenience store shelf.

People call me the *'Overtime King.'* I did not ask for the title, but I know why it stuck. I rarely say no to extra shifts, not because I love being busy, but because I know what it feels like to come up short. Every shift carried a name. School fees. Medication. A social security payment. Survival translated into hours. I have missed more holidays than I can count. Some days, I felt like I knew the rhythm of hospital machines better than my own family's voices.

We do not talk enough about how the OFW experience bends your sense of self.

The weight is not only financial. It is emotional. You love deeply, yet you are never sure if you are enough. You are celebrated for your sacrifices, then expected to keep sacrificing. The applause is loudest when you stay silent about your exhaustion. Inspiring to others. Rarely asked if you are okay.

Sometimes, being an OFW felt like the longest season of Survivor. No tribes. No torches. Just endurance. Every shift a challenge. Every remittance a vote to stay in the game. You smile through scarcity. Read moods like strategy maps. Outlast your own exhaustion. There are no immunity idols. Only the hope that if you keep showing up, visibly useful and quietly excellent, you will not be the one voted out of the dream.

That is the contract. Survive beautifully, but do not disturb the structure. The story works better when you are grateful and exhausted. Not when you ask why it costs so much.

I kept showing up. Because that is what we do.

—

Filipino history is full of heroes. The lone figure who endures. The one who sacrifices so others survive. It is a beautiful inheritance. It is also a dangerous one.

When you grow up believing salvation comes from one strong figure, you learn to wait for rescue instead of building systems. Loyalty before scrutiny. Gratitude before accountability. Sometimes that instinct leads us to place our hopes in leaders who promise protection but deliver spectacle. We confuse endurance with virtue. Suffering with moral proof.

That logic does not only shape politics. It shapes lives.
We learn to carry more than is fair. To stay silent longer than is healthy. To keep giving because that is what heroes do. Slowly, survival stops being a phase and becomes an identity.

Behind the noble sheen of hard work sits another reality. *Guilt.*
I felt guilty for wanting things. For spending on myself. For imagining a life not built entirely around sacrifice. When Nanay visited me in Australia, we argued about what to send home. I wanted her to buy better groceries. New shoes. She refused. Her instinct was always to give, even if it meant going without.
That instinct became mine.

For years, I delayed joy. Rest. Romance. Self-kindness. My longest relationship was with a to do list. While others dated, I managed two lives, two currencies, two careers. It was not martyrdom. It was survival.

And survival has a price.

I learned slowly and painfully that you cannot give your best when you are barely holding yourself together. Nobody warns you how much you lose when you never pause. Or how disorienting it feels when you finally do.

Investing in myself felt illicit at first. Almost selfish. I went back to school. Took exams that cost more than some people's monthly rent. Built a business, not for status, but to create something that would not vanish the moment I stopped working. This was not choosing ambition over family. It was choosing not to disappear while helping everyone else survive.

Still, envy crept in. I resented how hard everything felt. Especially when others chased dreams without checking exchange rates or visa rules first. Some days, I wondered if staying *'just'* a nurse would have been simpler. Less paperwork. More sleep.

But I could not settle. Not from ingratitude, but because I knew I had more to give. And that came at a cost.

I once stood in a rental kitchen, cold in winter and damp in summer, wishing I could afford the apartment I wanted. Nothing luxurious. Just clean. Safe. Warm. But the difference in rent meant no savings. No tuition. No remittances. So I wore extra socks. Cooked on Sundays. Reheated leftovers all week. Over time, I learned the point of working hard is not only to escape scarcity. It is to change the story. To build success that allows rest. That offers choice. That includes *you*.

Becoming, I realized, meant not just building a future, but making sure I was allowed to live in it. Rewriting the story required naming the old one. The one that rewards self-erasure and calls it honor.

Here is the paradox. The qualities that made my family strong are the same ones I now must loosen my grip on.

I carry deep gratitude for what my culture taught me. To give without keeping score. To love through action more than words. That generosity built entire futures. But even sacred traits become heavy when you are never allowed to set them down.

I do not want to live where joy must be justified. I want to believe that spending on memories is not indulgent, but instructive. That investing in rest, in books, in therapy, in decent shoes is not selfish. It is wise.

I still send money home. I still work long hours. But I also rest. Save. Make room for joy. Not as a reward, but as a right.

Sometimes it looks like a hot meal I did not reheat. Or a book I will never finish. Or buying the good shampoo.

What surprised me most was not achievement, but how much of my effort had been spent surviving rules I never agreed to. Financial responsibility is not just paying bills. It is paying attention. To limits. To dreams. To the person you are becoming.

Over time, survival stopped being the only goal. I did not just want to escape scarcity. I wanted to interrupt it. There is a difference between sending money home and sending knowledge forward. One keeps people afloat. The other teaches them how to stay upright when the tide turns.

I began explaining what I learned the hard way. How contracts work. How visas expire. How interest compounds against you. How systems reward those who understand the rules early. I showed family how to manage money. Friends how to plan before leaping. Younger nurses how to ask better questions before signing anything that promised opportunity and delivered exhaustion. Not because I had it all figured out. Because I knew what it cost not to.

Paying it forward was not charity. It was strategy with a conscience. Teaching others did not make me poorer. It made the water less hostile.

Maybe that is the evolution of the dream. Not just climbing out, but reaching back with clearer hands. Not just surviving, but multiplying options for those coming next. That, too, has a cost. Time. Patience. Emotional labor. But it costs far less than silence.

Some days, I still feel the price in the security I postponed, the vacations I skipped, the love I missed. But those costs were not wasted. They were investments.

This is what it means to chase a dream without wealth or safety nets. You do not just work for it. You stretch. You sacrifice. You hope it adds up.

Even when the math does not make sense, you keep going. Because you are not just building a life. You are building a different future.

And just when I thought resilience had to be inconspicuous, she arrived — loud, brilliant, and unbothered. *Captain Carmel.*

Soul Notes

❖ When was the last time you let yourself *want more* without apology or justification?

❖ What dream have you shelved in the name of duty and is it still waiting for you?

❖ Who does your hustle serve and are *you* included in the return on investment?

Chapter 20: Captain Carmel

After years of running on ambition and caffeine, I didn't expect my next breakthrough to smell like my mother.

I was still deep in the grind. Overtimes, multiple currencies, rationing joy like it came with a receipt.

Making friends as an adult is a peculiar, often suspicious ritual. It's like dating minus the candlelight and with more talk about rosters, taxes, and whether this mole looks *'normal'*. And in a hospital, that swirling cauldron of adrenaline, sarcasm, and industrial-strength hand sanitizer, it's trickier still.

When you're a migrant nurse, the calculus changes again. Migration scatters your people like dandelion seeds. One week, the ward hums with accents from Dublin, Delhi, and Durban; the next, half the team is gone. Contracts end, visas expire, life chapters close abruptly. Loneliness is the part no one puts on the recruitment brochures. The way you can be surrounded by colleagues and still feel unmoored, your closest friends reduced to names on a WhatsApp thread that goes silent over time.

You learn to keep a polite distance. Enough warmth to work well together, but not so much that goodbye will gut you. Psychologists might call it emotional self-preservation. I called it *cordial disengagement*.

I'd learned the cost in New Zealand. My closest friends were gone within months. Contracts ending, visas denied, careers pulled elsewhere. One day you're sharing midnight toast after a shift; the next, waving at their airport gate, both pretending you'll visit soon. You mean it at the time. But migration has its own gravity.

Hospitals only deepen that churn. They run on shortages, plugging gaps with an international workforce expected to adapt overnight. To new hierarchies, unspoken rules, cultural nuances. By the time I moved to Australia, I was fluent in the migrant nurse survival kit: smile, adapt, don't expect permanence. Even in a new city, the cycle was the same. Colleagues gone as quickly as they came, rosters shifting like tides.

In that pattern, migrants often cluster with those who share their language or heritage. It's one less thing to translate. But that safety can also become a cage. Your circle limited to sameness when the real gift of migration is meeting people you never would've crossed paths with otherwise.

In Wellington, I'd found *whānau* at work. People who felt like home. But even that was temporary, scattered by geography and life's unrelenting pull. I'd stopped expecting to feel that again. And then, every now and then, someone cuts through all of that.

For me, that someone was *Captain Carmel*. An Irish green in the middle of my Filipino tropics, both of us rooted unexpectedly under Australian skies.

I noticed her first not for what she said, but for how she smelled. Exactly like Nanay. The scent of childhood mornings, freshly ironed uniforms, gentle strength. It cracked something open in me. Before I knew her name, I knew I'd love her. It was as if Nanay's memory had sent a scout ahead. To remind me I wasn't as alone as I thought.

And I was right.

Carmel is what happens when a nurse, a saint, and your funniest older cousin walk into a bar. And walk out as one magnificent being. She listens with her whole face. Laughs like joy is a vitamin deficiency she's committed to curing. Comforts like a weighted blanket. Her presence doesn't command attention, it *grounds* you.

I called her Captain Carmel not because she barks orders (she doesn't), but because she could lift both your spirits and a fully stocked supply trolley. Radiant, strong, and somehow still up for the gym after night shift. Her strength is both physical and moral, and neither is accidental. If the hospital caught fire, she'd be calmly leading the way, coordinating chaos, and still cracking a joke about how the alarm sounds like a vintage Nokia ringtone.

She's the kind of person who doesn't just enter your life — she *joins* it.

At the bedside, where masks fall away and the core of a person shows up, Carmel shines. You learn a lot about people there. Whether they're performing or truly present. Whether they treat patients like puzzles or like people.

And Carmel?

She's gentle with patients and firm with injustice. She has the best bedside manner I've seen — empathetic, honest, present. No theatrics. Just the rare kind of stillness that makes you feel safe without needing to ask.

She *sees* the human every single time: consultants, interns, cleaners, patients. You're not your title to her. You're your tenderness. She doesn't take herself too seriously, but she takes her patients seriously. That's the difference. That's the magic.

That's rare in any workplace. In a hospital powered by migrant labor, it's rare to find two shades of green — hers, deep and mossy; mine, bright and sunlit — growing in the same garden and flourishing anyway.

We often arrive carrying the weight of being *'the outsider'*. Not just in a country, but sometimes in our own teams. Carmel's way of seeing bypasses all of that. She doesn't flatten differences. She honors them, meeting people where they are without the transactional edge that shadows so many workplace relationships.

She's the *Angelina Jolie of the Animal Kingdom* minus the bodyguards, plus the chew toys. Bailey and Milo are her pampered canines, and if a friend goes overseas, she'll adopt their pets too. She talks to dogs like they're visiting dignitaries and dresses them like French royalty.

And when you're a migrant, navigating loneliness, estrangement, time zones that betray your sense of family, that kind of seeing matters. Migration can make you feel like your life is on pause until you secure the next visa, find a partner, or buy a home you don't just rent. Carmel made me realize belonging isn't something you wait for. It's something you create in real time, with whoever is brave enough to meet you there.

We built a friendship not on intensity, but on consistency. She's the kind of friend who'll give you her last pair of contact lenses because she knows you can't read the cardiac monitor without them. Who'll laugh with you over memes and cry with you in the supply closet when life hits too hard.

Once, she got a ring stuck on her finger during a shift. It swelled, turned purple, refused to budge. Most people would've panicked. Carmel just smiled, made jokes all the way to the Emergency Room, and charmed the firemen as they sawed it off. Pain but laced with punchlines. That's her way.

We've saved lives together. Rolled our eyes across a ward in perfect sync. Survived night shift bureaucracy with nothing but caffeine, music, and each other's wit. And here's the wildest thing: *I didn't even know I was missing her until I met her.*

Bella, my 6-year-old niece, declared before she'd even met her, *"Aunty Carmel is my best friend."* Kids don't wait for evidence. They feel the *energy*, and trust it. That's the purest kind of knowing. One that doesn't need logic to catch up.

Carmel is Irish. I've never set foot in Ireland. But with her, it felt like I came home to something. Kindness has no postcode. Migration taught me that connection isn't about finding replicas of yourself. In Brazil, Berlin, Boston — the people who felt most like home rarely looked like me or spoke my first language. Carmel was proof it could happen in a fluorescent-lit ward in Sydney.

I used to think being unpartnered meant something was missing. But some loves, like friendship, arrive already whole.

Carmel reminded me of that.

In all her unassuming glory, she made space for me — the nurse, the lawyer, the wandering heart — and did it not with fanfare. With a well-timed joke. With the unexpected smell of my mother. With a kind of goodness that feels unshakable.

She reminded me that hope isn't naïve — it's a discipline. Every time you choose to believe in people, you give them the chance to prove you right.

She is proof that in a world of contracts, rosters, and shifting allegiances, there are still good people. And if you keep your eyes open, your heart soft, and your sarcasm sharp, you just might find them.

And if you're lucky? You get to call one of them Captain —
preferably one who carries snacks in her scrub pocket and doesn't
judge your caffeine intake.

—

In the thick of chasing dreams and dodging burnout, she reminded
me. What grounds you isn't just purpose — it's people. And in
migration's constant motion, those people become your anchor
points. They're proof that even when your postcode changes, your
circle can still grow. If you're willing to risk the ache of goodbye
for the joy of belonging.

I'd spent years being strong for everyone else. But strength without
softness isn't sustainable. Eventually, I stopped trying to build a
fortress and started searching for a rhythm. Not just a routine. A
rebellion.

Sabbath became my way back. Not to religion, but to myself.

And on the days I forget — the scent of Nanay, carried by a friend
whose green is nothing like mine yet thrives just as wildly here — is
enough to remind me. To keep looking for the good, because it's
always closer than I think.

Soul Notes

❖ Who reminded you that goodness still exists just by showing up
with kindness?

❖ Which friendship in your life feels less like coincidence, and
more like *chosen kin?*

❖ What do people feel in your presence — seen, soothed,
stretched, or something else entirely?

Chapter 21: Sabbaths of the Soul

*"Sometimes you don't need to get away.
You just need to come back to yourself."*

When I was younger, I read *Chicken Soup for the Soul.*

They were bite-sized essays. Small human stories that somehow held big truths. I didn't always grasp the moral, but I knew how they made me feel — cracked open, seen, softened. That was my first education in empathy. A schooling in how to listen for life beneath the noise.

Looking back, I've always been drawn to stories that reach below the surface. Not just the kind that tell you what happened, but the kind that dare to ask what it means. That's what I mean when I say soul — not something lofty or religious — but something that notices. That pauses. That dares to make meaning out of moments others rush past.

To me, the soul is the part of us that watches from the edges. The out-of-body observer, the discreet philosopher. The one that doesn't just move through the day but wonders what the day is trying to teach. It doesn't always speak, but it listens. It remembers. It holds space for what's tender and true, even after the world has moved on.

And that's what this chapter is: A *sabbath.*

Not just a rest from labor, but a return to self. A deliberate pause to check in with the part of me that doesn't just do — but *feels.* Notices. Connects.

The part that still believes rest is sacred. Beauty is necessary. And that slowing down isn't quitting but remembering who you are when you're not performing for anyone.

—

I came to the law later than most. While my peers were clerking and networking in their twenties, I was wearing scrubs and doing 12-hour shifts. By the time I earned my second degree and passed the bar, I wasn't just building a practice, I was trying to reclaim lost time.

So, I moved fast. Too fast.

There was always a sense that I had to catch up. That I had to prove I belonged. Not just as a lawyer, but as someone who'd taken the long road there. I was trying to hit every milestone before forty. Trying, without realizing it, to punish myself for the circumstances that delayed me in the first place.
Rest wasn't just inconvenient. It felt disloyal to the hunger that got me here.

For most of my adult life, I treated rest like an afterthought. Something you earned only when everything else was handled. When the patients were discharged. The files were closed. The emails answered. The lists conquered.

Of course, that moment never came. So rest became a mirage I kept chasing. Something I deferred to *'later.'*

By the time I was working full-time as an ICU nurse while building a U.S. immigration law practice from Sydney, I had become extremely good at high functioning. My life was color-coded across three time zones. I knew exactly how much sleep I could go without and still operate at 80 percent. I could support a patient through cardiac arrest in the morning and counsel a client through a visa petition by mid-afternoon. I was balancing lives and laws. I was doing it all.

For a while, I mistook exhaustion for evidence. I thought being perpetually tired meant I was doing something right. That the weight I carried somehow proved my worth. The more I endured, the more it felt like I was winning. Or at least, surviving with style. I didn't just wear overwork; I weaponized it. In doing so, I called it discipline when it was really depletion.

There was no collapse. No Emergency Room visit. Just a slow erosion. Meals eaten standing up. Walks traded for Zooms. Joy shelved. Beauty ignored. I didn't feel like I was failing, but I was fading.

The cost wasn't just physical. It was existential.
I was disappearing from my own life.

And what made it more absurd — and more heartbreaking — was that I was living in Sydney. A city people daydream about. A place with surf breaks in one direction, wine regions in the other, and national parks running right through its ribs. Where weekends are supposed to taste like fish and chips by the wharf, smell like sunscreen on salty skin, and sound like seagulls fighting over your leftovers.

And I wasn't enjoying any of it.

My apartment wasn't far from beaches that made magazine covers, but my calendar never left room to visit them. I'd walk past cafés full of people sipping oat lattés in activewear, looking like they had time to spare, and I'd be speed-walking to the train, already behind on the next task. On the rare days I wasn't working, I'd still be thinking about work, fielding after-hours emails.

While tourists marveled at sandstone cliffs and harbor views, I was refreshing search tabs as the light outside shifted golden. While others dipped into the ocean at Bronte or wandered barefoot through Watsons Bay, I was toggling between patient charts and visa briefs, always trying to get ahead, stay ahead, outrunning the feeling that I was already behind.

It's one thing to be tired in a city you don't care about.
It's another thing to feel numb inside a place that's meant to be full of life.

I thought of an old acquaintance I once ran into at a hospital. Someone I knew years ago who had become a partner at a private equity firm. One of those people who lived on planes and deadlines, whose calendar was always full. He was in treatment for cancer. We didn't speak for long, but I remember him saying, *"I worked every day of my life. I blinked, and it was over. I don't think I ever really enjoyed any of it."*

He wasn't bitter. Just… bewildered. Like he'd followed all the rules, only to realize he'd missed the point.

And I thought of Auntie Belen. The same aunt I visited in San Francisco whose life was defined by work. A nurse in the United States — hardworking, dependable, the kind of person who never complained and rarely paused. She worked back-to-back shifts, sent money home, put others ahead of herself without hesitation. She always assumed that one day she'd slow down, take a break, maybe finally enjoy the life she'd spent so long building.

But that day never came. Cancer arrived quickly. She never got her later.

Two different people. Two different lives. But the same lesson. Even the strongest among us can run out of time before we learn how to rest.

I know I'm ambitious. Always have been. But I don't want to build something meaningful at the cost of missing the *meaning*. I don't want to be so focused on what I'm becoming that I forget to be *here* for it.

Somewhere in the hustle and bustle of daily life, between shift handovers and sentence revisions, I began to forget. Forget that there was once a version of me who moved slower. Who found stillness sacred. Who listened to the hum of nature like it was an old friend. I remembered it again on quiet days, in flashes — the hush of dawn on the Kepler Track, the moss-covered calm of the Routeburn, the ancient stillness of the Larapinta Trail.

Some Sabbaths didn't look like Sunday mornings. They looked like burnt-orange dust underfoot and stars so close they made you whisper. Like the Larapinta Trail, where silence stretched wider than grief and each step hummed with something older than ambition. That one stayed with me, especially. Unlike the alpine trails of New Zealand, Larapinta was sun-scorched and unapologetic — raw, ochre-hued, and deeply Australian. It reminded me that this land, too, could hold me. That presence doesn't always come in lushness. Sometimes it's found in dust, in silence, in standing still while everything else rushes.

And then, one overbooked weekday, I bailed on everything and took the ferry to Manly.

I didn't plan it. I just needed air. The ferry ride alone felt like a full body reset. That Sydney Harbour sparkle always manages to look deliberate. The sun hit the water like it had something to prove. Kids were licking ice creams with Olympic-level commitment.

Even the seagulls looked smug. Manly didn't feel like self-care. It felt like self-respect.

I stepped off and wandered past sun-drenched joggers and wet golden retrievers, letting the salt wind undo me. Roller's Bakehouse had a croissant that felt like a religious experience — warm, golden, unapologetically buttery.

Later, I slipped into the rock pool at the edge of the beach. My body sank into the cold water like it remembered something before I did. I didn't think about the hospital. I didn't think about the practice. I just floated. I just existed.

That was the start.

Then came the Coogee to Bondi Walk, a stretch of coastline I'd done before, but always at pace. This time, I let it move me. The ocean was roaring. Waves smashed against cliffs like punctuation. You don't overthink your to-do list when you're standing in front of that kind of force. You just stand there, reminded of your smallness. And your *aliveness*.

I didn't know it then, but I was recalibrating.

Sydney doesn't nudge you toward presence. It demands it. With salt wind, with sunlight, with seagulls which do not believe in boundaries. It doesn't whisper; it dazzles. It's not trying to be poetic. It just is. Brash and brilliant and unbothered by your KPIs. And if you're lucky enough to notice, it will knock the breath out of you.

The Opera House did the same. I'd rushed past it dozens of times. But the first time I sat inside the Concert Hall, something shifted. Stepping inside it is like entering a space designed not just for sound, but for silence. The air changes. Cooler. Denser. There's a hush that comes from reverence. The timber panels curve like the ribs of a giant wooden whale, warm-toned and acoustically perfect. You can feel the design in how your footsteps soften against the red carpet, how your breath seems to pause when you look up. The ceiling feels impossibly high, and yet somehow intimate, like it's listening. Even before the music starts, your body knows that everything ordinary has just stepped outside.

The Sydney Symphony Orchestra opened with Brahms. The room hushed itself. The kind of silence that feels shared. The kind that settles your bones. For a few moments, the audience — hundreds of us — inhaled together. I don't remember every piece they played. I just remember the feeling that someone had cracked open my chest and let the music pour straight in.

And strangely, as the violins swelled, I found myself thinking about *Brahmsstraße*, the street I once lived on in Germany. Back then, I hadn't yet connected the name to the man. But now, seated in the grandeur of the Sydney Opera House, I realized that this music had once walked the same cobbled ground I had. Brahms, one of Germany's revered *'Three Bs'* alongside Bach and Beethoven — a holy trinity of sound and soul — was no longer just a composer to me. He was a memory. A street sign. A mood.

To think I'd once rushed past his name on my way to a train station. And now, his music was slowing me down, reminding me of all the things I used to ignore in pursuit of progress.
Funny how meaning waits for us. Sometimes in concert halls. Sometimes in street names. Always in hindsight.

A week later, I was back. This time for Chaka Khan, whose soul and funk filled the same space that had once held sonatas. It was as divine as it was defiant. Brilliance doesn't have a dress code. It just needs room.

At the Joan Sutherland Theatre, I sobbed through *La Traviata*, laughed out loud during *The Barber of Seville*, and sat still through crescendos that left me breathless. Opera doesn't apologize for its emotions. It lets them take up space. That night, watching heartbreak unfold in Italian while wearing my best attempt at semi-formal attire, I remembered that you don't need to understand every lyric to feel every note.

That's what beauty does. It interrupts the performance of coping and invites something *deeper*.

And then there was sleep, the sabbath I neglected most of all. I had convinced myself there was no time to rest properly, that if I wasn't awake, I wasn't *'being productive.'* But sleep, like all forms of rest, is sacred. It's a sabbath we often take for granted, when in fact, it's where the body and mind reconnect and rebuild. It's the reset that makes everything else possible.

I would collapse into bed, exhausted, unaware of how much I was depriving myself of something essential. It wasn't just the lack of hours at night; it was the quality of rest I was missing. The deep, nourishing sleep that restores energy and focus. I was missing the sabbath that would allow me to truly be present in my life.

Rest didn't just soften me. It disarmed the weapon I once called work.

It reminded me that worth isn't proven in pain.
That presence is not the prize — it's the point.

There's a particular kind of grief that comes with realizing you've become functional at the expense of being human. But there's also a kind of grace that returns when you start noticing again.

We're shaped by a world that confuses efficiency with excellence. We've built systems — professional, educational, economic — that value output over insight, busy-ness over depth. Everywhere you look, people are measuring their worth in units of productivity.

We wear exhaustion like a badge. We schedule our lives to the minute and call it discipline. Stillness has been reframed as laziness. Beauty as a luxury. Rest as weakness. And somewhere in that calculus, we're losing something essential. The ability to feel deeply, to notice what's good, to be fully *here*.

I used to think adventure only looked like passports and productivity and high-stakes choices. But I've learned that the most noble adventures sometimes ask you to be still. Not as a retreat from your ambition, but as a way of grounding it. Presence doesn't derail the journey. It reminds you why you started.

I didn't quit. I didn't downsize. I didn't become someone else. I started living *with* myself — not chasing past or future versions of me.

I used to think the goal was to arrive. In a new country, a new role, a new version of myself. I thought if I could just land somewhere impressive enough, I'd finally feel grounded. That certainty would follow achievement. That wholeness would follow titles.

So I hustled — not just toward progress, but toward proof. Every milestone became a checkpoint: a degree, a job title, a visa, a lease in a postcode I once couldn't afford.

I kept thinking: *If I do enough, maybe the ache will pacify.*

But it didn't. It just changed shape. From urgency to perfectionism. From impostor syndrome to over-functioning.

I told myself I was chasing arrival. But what I was really chasing
was permission.

Permission to stop running.
To rest without guilt.
To want softness in a world that rewards grit.
To exist — not as a performance, but as a person.

I kept waiting for someone to hand it to me. A mentor, a
milestone, a moment that would say,
"You've made it. You can exhale now."

But that permission?
I could've given it to myself the whole time.

—

Rest, I've learned, must be real. It's not something you earn after
the burnout. It's what might keep you from burning out in the first
place.

*Even the most noble and honorable pursuits — the law, the healing, the
building of something that matters — can't be sustained without moments of
sabbath along the way.*

Because a life built on purpose is only half the equation.
The other half is knowing how to stay awake to it.

These sabbaths of the soul — the pauses, the pleasures, the places
that remind you you're human — aren't distractions from the
noble and honorable adventures.

They *are* the noble and honorable adventures.

A croissant in Manly. A sea breeze on your skin. A soprano in full heartbreak. These moments don't pull you away from your purpose; they stitch you more tightly to it.

The challenge isn't just to keep going. It's to keep feeling. To keep noticing. To keep choosing presence even when productivity tries to seduce you into forgetting yourself.

Sabbaths taught me how to pause. To be still, to be tender, to be held by something greater than achievement. But after learning to rest, I also had to learn to play. After all, healing doesn't only come in peaceful moments. Sometimes, it's also in the laughter that follows the silence.

Soul Notes

❖ When was the last time you did something purely for joy to *feel* alive?

❖ What small pleasure reminds you that rest isn't a reward but a right?

❖ If your younger self could plan your next day off, what would they make sure you didn't forget?

❖ What permission have you been waiting for that only you can give?

Chapter 22: Stoic with a Sense of Humor

"Life is too important to be taken seriously."
— Oscar Wilde

After learning how to pause, I had to learn how to play.

If sabbath taught me how to reclaim stillness in a world obsessed with speed, humor taught me how to reclaim lightness in a world obsessed with composure.

Humor, in my case, came in parallel with Stoicism.

Stoicism is often misunderstood as cold detachment, while humor thrives on emotional release. But together, interestingly, they offer a steady foundation — strength and lightness coexisting — helping me rise through life's absurdity with grounding.

First: humor.

By now, I've collected enough degrees, stamps, and sleepless nights to know that striving without soul is just burnout dressed up as ambition. It's not the hours that undo you. It's the absence of lightness between them. Discipline, when divorced from joy, stops being strength and becomes self-punishment disguised as virtue.

And if I took everything seriously, I'd have burned out by now — buried beneath bureaucracy, grief, and the sheer absurdity of life as a nurse-lawyer-migrant navigating systems never built for people like me.

But I haven't always been light.

For the longest time, I thought seriousness was the price of competence. We were taught to wear composure like a badge. To furrow brows in the name of brilliance. To assume the one who laughs least is the one most in control.

And I bought into that myth. Hard.

I thought lightness meant weakness. That humor made me forgettable. That to be taken seriously, I had to act like someone who never laughed too loudly. Or cried during Pixar movies.

Part of that came from survival. As a migrant navigating multiple roles, I wore gravitas like armor. I didn't want to give people another reason not to take me seriously. Humor felt risky. Levity felt like luxury.

The world — with its stiff dress codes and gatekeepers — didn't disagree. Being *'put-together'* meant composed. The safest bet was silence. And that, I could put together.

Growing up, I was taught that strength meant silence. Dignity meant endurance. You never joked around elders, and you certainly didn't laugh when life was busy smacking you in the face. Humor was a luxury we couldn't afford. We bore hardship without complaint.

I remember Nanay receiving bad news with a face carved in stone. Not a flicker of emotion. I learned then that strength was the ability to hold everything in.

But adulthood revealed something different. Humor — however risky — became a lifeline. Not an escape from pain, but a way to carry it. When suffering became heavy, humor allowed me to stay standing. Even if it meant breaking the rules I grew up with.

And life — especially in the ICU and in law — made sure I had plenty of practice.

"They say laughter is the best medicine. Unless you're in the ICU — in which case, please administer actual medicine."

There was a night shift I'll never forget. I was running late, exhaustion dragging behind me like a second body. I stepped into the elevator and stood beside a teary-eyed patient's relative. The silence was thick. The air, heavy with unspoken grief. And then I cracked a joke about my tardiness. Her laugh — surprised and relieved — cut through the tension like sunlight through clouds. For a moment, our roles weren't nurse and family member. We were just two tired humans sharing a flicker of light in a dark place.

It reminded me of those viral Nurse John skits — ridiculous, sharp, uncomfortably accurate. There's truth in the comedy. Humor doesn't distract from the heaviness. It acknowledges it without drowning in it.

"Justice is blind — but if you're in court, it might also be hard of hearing. So, please speak clearly and don't forget the evidence."

Once, a self-represented litigant told the judge, *"Your Honor, I didn't bring evidence because I thought my honesty would be enough."* It was the legal equivalent of bringing vibes to a knife fight. The judge, deadpan, replied, *"This isn't Judge Judy, sir. We need paperwork."* That's what I admire — dignity and wit. The ability to be firm and kind, with a wink.

That moment stayed with me because it revealed something deeper. The courtroom wasn't just a stage for rules and rhetoric. It was a place where personality, presence, and even a little humor could soften the sharp edges of justice. But I didn't always believe I belonged there.

I used to think I wasn't cut out for law. I wasn't white, I wasn't 6'5", I didn't have blonde hair or blue eyes — the kind of *'successful'* man they portray in legal dramas. I was more of a *'local flavor'* — a little darker, a little shorter, with hair that looked like it had survived a few too many 3 a.m. drafting sessions. In rooms filled with crisp suits and stiffer smiles, I felt like a suit that didn't fit — too loud, too soft, too something.

But in my gut, I knew I was not meant to fit a mold. I was meant to melt it down and build something better.

I started loving myself more. Because it turns out, being a lawyer isn't about looking like the poster. It's about knowing the law. And knowing yourself.

In hindsight, it wasn't just about credibility. It was about fear — the recurrent kind. The kind that follows you through visa queues and unspoken rules, whispering, *"Don't mess this up. They're watching."*

But humor helped me walk through those moments anyway. Not by escaping the pressure, but by making space to breathe through it. And that's what humor became — my *quiet fire* — the slow burn of resilience and the warmth that keeps you going when it's just you and your will to keep showing up.

It burned through ICU nights and legal deadlines. Through grief and joy. Through fear and fatigue.

And then, with that fire, came Stoicism.

Not as emotional suppression, but to hold steady when everything else trembled.

Seneca said, *"We suffer more in imagination than in reality."*

Epictetus was basically the ancient Greek version of *"Control what you can, laugh at what you can't, and don't engage with trolls on Twitter."*

Marcus Aurelius wrote, *"You have power over your mind and not over outside events."* That became my mantra in rooms where pain or panic tried to take over. In emergencies, Stoicism steadied me. In grief, it pacified me. In law, it anchored me. In all those moments, I wasn't just a professional. I was someone learning how to hold chaos without becoming it.

Humor gave me air. Stoicism gave me spine.
Together, they didn't shield me from storms; they taught me how to dance in the rain.

I still write serious emails — but I sneak in a cheeky PS.
I still carry grief — but I tuck in a punchline when I can.
I still suit up, show up, and hold it all together.

Because life's too short to wear starch without soul. The world throws chaos your way — delays, grief, rejection, powerlessness. Sometimes all at once. You don't get to pick the weather. But you can choose how you meet it.

With grit. With grace. With a good joke.

Because carrying life's weight doesn't always mean standing still. Sometimes it means moving forward, even when the wind insists otherwise.

Some days I ride my bike through Sydney's coastal winds, fighting every gust. The wind doesn't care. It just pushes. Stoicism lets me lean into it. Humor adds the tailwind that helps me smile through it.

If you're not a Stoic, everything feels like an attack. Even a buffering Zoom call. If you don't have humor, you forget how to laugh when you're not the punchline. And if you have neither, you'll collapse. Not because you're weak, but because you were never taught how to bend.

Stoicism and humor won't erase the weight.
But they'll help you carry it.

They are my quiet fire — fierce, steady, and still burning.

Because in this life, survival isn't always about being loud or fast.
Sometimes, it's about walking through the storm with a smile.

Soul Notes

❖ How has humor shaped your ability to navigate your toughest times?

❖ In moments of chaos or uncertainty, how do you draw on stillness or lightness to steady yourself?

Chapter 23: We Who Carry Quiet Fire

Tatay once drew a triangle in the dirt: oxygen, fuel, heat.
"That's how fire begins," he said.

I didn't know then that this simple lesson would one day explain my own life.

We live in a world that rewards volume. Confidence is often mistaken for competence. Visibility is treated as value. But becoming does not always require spectacle. Some strengths burn softly, behind lanyards and lunchboxes, inside library books and hospital corridors. They are fierce not in flash, but in endurance.

In the last chapter, I leaned on Stoicism and humor, two unlikely allies that helped me survive ambition's chaos. But somewhere between levity and logic, I sensed the need for something deeper. A kind of strength that persists after the punchline fades. That stays when cleverness and calm run out.

That is where *quiet fire* comes in.
This chapter is for the ones who keep going without applause.

For years, I confused exhaustion with progress. ICU night shifts bled into study mornings. Law deadlines followed me into hospital corridors. I reviewed contracts on lunch breaks that never quite arrived. I learned to survive on short naps, long to-do lists, and the belief that rest was something I could earn later.

Loneliness crept in between time zones. Friends slept while I worked. Family calls were squeezed between shifts. Some nights it felt like I existed only in transit, between wards, between countries, between versions of myself.

I told myself this was strength. But fire without oxygen doesn't last.

What I fed myself was urgency, adrenaline, obligation. It burned hot, but shallow. Eventually my body noticed. So did my spirit. Years later, while juggling critical care and building a law practice across borders, I returned to Tatay's triangle. Burnout, fatigue, and self-doubt all pointed to the same truth: *fire needs tending*.

It wasn't ambition that carried me through lonely library nights and sterile hospital corridors. It was something more serene. Showing up. Choosing to breathe. Choosing to stay.

I started seeing it everywhere. In single mothers pushing prams to nursing school. In migrants relearning professions in foreign languages. In carers who kept showing up without being asked. This kind of strength rarely demands recognition, but it deserves remembrance. More than charisma or credentials, it is what keeps people moving forward when the world is not looking.

To carry this fire is to choose identity. It is deciding not to let noise dictate worth. I felt this most clearly during the years I held both scrubs and contracts in my bag, moving between wards and conference rooms, learning that survival and selfhood could coexist.

Quiet fire meant continuing, not for validation, but because I was building something — *someone* — that could last.

—

For a long time, I believed power had to be loud. That leadership meant commanding rooms and exiting with credit.

Quiet fire taught me otherwise.

For people like us, migrants, carers, builders of modest lives, the work often happens offstage. We start behind. An unfamiliar name can stall an interview. An accent can decide credibility. The system does not always reject you outright. Sometimes it simply overlooks you. You learn early how to carry more, explain more, prove more.

I grew up watching people hold families together without recognition. Duty came before dreams. Survival before self-expression. I once mistook volume for strength and admired leaders who could silence rooms, mistaking intimidation for authority. It took years to understand that real leadership does not need to dominate. The people who shaped me most were not the loudest. They were steady. They showed up consistently. They earned trust calmly.

That was when I realized that becoming is not about commanding attention. It is about standing firm in your worth.

I learned about Erlinda Espiritu through LinkedIn, a platform better known for corporate clichés than revelation. Born during war and occupation, she became one of the first women lawyers in the Philippines in 1947, and by 1951, the first Filipina to earn a law degree from Harvard. There was no spectacle. Just discipline, dignity, and decades of impact.

Sometimes leadership does not announce itself. Sometimes it simply walks ahead and makes space.

Cecille carries that same gravity. In a suburban home stacked with textbooks and toys, she raised three children alone while building a law practice from scratch. Dinner, homework, bedtime. Client calls between school runs. Watching her taught me that endurance does not harden you. It deepens you.

I see it too in Ronald, who turns bank jargon into lifelines for migrants, always steady, always patient. In Naj, whose leadership arrives with conviction and warmth, often carrying his Ina's *pastil,* reminding you that justice does not have to be cold to be firm. I see it in the hospital janitor who treats floors like sacred ground. In the shopkeeper who remembers your name. In the stranger who offers directions in a language that is not theirs.

They are not glamorous. They are grounded. They do not measure success in headlines or titles, but in the lives they lift and the dignity they insist on.

I did not grow up believing people like us shaped history. Now I know we do, because we shape each other.

Not all torches blaze. Some simply keep the room lit long enough for someone else to find their way.

—

I once auditioned for MasterChef Australia twice and did not make it. What I wanted was not a trophy, but visibility for Filipino cuisine, rich, layered, rooted in history, yet still underrepresented globally. So, when Chef Miko Aspiras appeared as guest judge at the Season 17 finale, weaving native Australian ingredients into Filipino flavors, it felt cultural, not just culinary. Innovation without erasure. Belonging without apology.

It mirrored something in me too. A reminder that integration does not require disappearance. That you can carry your roots forward while still evolving.

Quiet fire does not have to abandon its origins to be seen. I want more Filipinos, and all *'others,'* to have that choice too. Not just to survive unseen, but to step forward when they are ready. Our humility should not be mistaken for inability. Our brilliance should not stay hidden simply because we learned to endure without recognition.

Quiet giants will always exist. But the world is richer when they also have the safety to take up space and announce themselves.

Tatay's triangle taught me that fire needs oxygen. Life taught me it also needs choice. To rest or rise. To stay or shine. And perhaps legacy is not in how long we burn, but in how many flames we help spark.

—

After years of practicing resilience, I felt a shift. Not away from duty, but toward discovery. For me, that spark arrived silently, not as revelation, but as permission. I learned to feed my fire with curiosity.

Quiet fire, given the right spark, stops merely surviving the dark. It begins to scan for light. It leans toward it. It dares to grow.

That is how survival becomes expansion.
That is where endurance meets *Eureka*.

Soul Notes

❖ What kind of fire are you carrying, and whose spark lit it?

❖ Who taught you that strength doesn't have to be loud to be lasting?

❖ What does legacy mean when no one is clapping, but you showed up anyway?

Chapter 24: Eureka

So, I followed it — the flicker, the question, the ache of not knowing.

I stopped reaching for answers and started reaching for air. For space to fumble and learn. Because becoming isn't just fire and forward motion. It's also play. Also pause. Slow unspooling of a mind brave enough to wonder.

There's a word I've always liked: *Eureka.* Most people know it as that moment of sudden insight, the kind that comes with wide eyes and an exclamation point. It's famously attributed to Archimedes, who purportedly shouted it after stepping into a bathtub and realizing water had shifted.

But not all revelations arrive with lightning. Some come as a nudge — inconvenient, irreversible. They require patience, curiosity, and intellectual humility, the willingness to admit you don't have the full picture yet, and to keep learning anyway. They arrive unscheduled, shifting the ground beneath everything that came before.

For me, Eureka moments weren't always a breakthrough, but an unshakable knowing. The path ahead had sharpened. A gear shift. A moment when I understood something differently than I did five minutes ago, and nothing after was the same.

—

As lawyers, we're trained in the art of argument. From the first day of law school, we're rewarded for spotting flaws, pouncing on loopholes, and crafting rebuttals sharp enough to draw blood. The adversarial mindset thrives, especially in common law systems. Winning, even by technicality, is often mistaken for mastery.

In my early years of practice, I clung tightly to that model. I approached contract negotiations like a sport. Every misplaced comma, every clumsy clause was an opportunity not to build a deal, but to score a point. I would highlight a typographical error in the recitals to prove I was paying attention. And I was. Just to the wrong things.

The wake-up call came not in the form of a courtroom defeat, but in something far subtler. A supervisor's *'chat.'* No raised voice. No dramatic dressing down. Just this:
"You're technically right," he said, *"but you're missing the point. Try being more commercial."*

I smiled, nodded, took notes, and spent the tram ride home muttering rebuttals under my breath.
"More commercial?"
My jaw set. But beneath the defensiveness was panic.
"What if he was right, and I didn't yet know how to be?"

Something in me bristled at what it asked of me. It wasn't about lowering standards but about enriching perspective. That being technically right wasn't always strategically wise. And that precision without purpose was just noise.

I began choosing my battles. I let go of the cosmetic errors and focused on the dealbreakers. Stopped trying to win every paragraph and started facilitating the win across the table. And then something strange happened. My metrics improved. My calendar breathed. Contracts closed faster. Revenue followed. Client satisfaction rose. Fewer firefights. Better solutions.

"Eureka!"

Law didn't have to be adversarial. At its best, it was collaborative. A bridge, not a battlefield. True mastery wasn't in defeating the other side, but in getting everyone across the finish line with dignity intact.

I had spent years trying to be the smartest person in the room. Then learned that the wisest one often speaks last, listens most, and lets a few small things slide in service of something bigger.

Being commercial wasn't about cutting corners. It was about elevating outcomes. Learning that didn't just make me a better lawyer. It trained me for the biggest negotiation of my life: *the one with myself.*

That was only the first. But life's turning points rarely arrive once.

One was hard. I failed the NCLEX on my first try. Years later, after passing the New York Bar, I saw it differently. It hadn't broken me. It had recalibrated me.

Some were spatial. As a migrant, subtle shifts stack before you feel at home. Walking along Circular Quay, it hit me. I wasn't shrinking anymore. I wasn't trying to belong. I simply did. Home wasn't about fitting in. It was about alignment.

Others came from integration. Moments when identities fused. I used to think my story had to fit a template. That people like me didn't shape systems, only survived them. While helping someone with a complex medical immigration issue, it all fused. I understood both the clinical language and the policy implications. My experience in healthcare made me a better advocate. I didn't have to choose between identities. They coexist, each enriching the other.

Some came from relentless effort forged in repetition and grit. During bar prep, buried in outlines and practice questions, I was convinced I was drowning. Nothing was sticking. Until I stopped trying to master everything and started trusting myself. Clarity didn't follow pressure. It followed release. I wasn't failing. I was forming.

And some came wrapped in beauty. After a week of ICU shifts, I sat at a Sydney Symphony concert. At the crescendo, I exhaled. I hadn't even realized I was holding my breath. Joy doesn't decorate life; it sustains it.

But the biggest Eureka? Opening ONOR Immigration Law.

It sounds inevitable now. But it wasn't. It felt radical. I was raised to be diligent, loyal. An excellent employee. Certainly not a founder. Our culture praises compliance over courage. But I was watching less-skilled people surge ahead not because they were better, but because they were *bolder.*

I knew I wasn't lacking ability, but I was outsourcing my power.

Launching ONOR Immigration Law wasn't just a career move or a business decision. It was reclamation. A refusal to wait to be chosen. A decision to choose myself. And through this work, help others do the same. It was the proof that I'd been listening to the voice tugging at me my whole life.

This moment was a permission slip. There was no formal *"Go ahead."* No masterclass telling me I was ready. In fact, I didn't feel ready at all. But I realized I was waiting for approval that would never come. Readiness isn't a milestone; it's a mindset. That realization gave me the courage to act, even if the circumstances weren't perfect. That voice had a name: *curiosity.*

Curiosity is the secret ingredient in every life shift. It's less a trait than a habit. The thing that makes you ask, *"What else is possible?"*

even when you're afraid. Curiosity doesn't promise certainty, but it makes discovery possible.

Sometimes it's *childlike wonder*. Like the first time I learned how the body works in nursing school or sat in awe inside a courtroom. Sometimes it's seeing the familiar with a *tourist's eyes* — falling in love again with Sydney's sandstone cliffs, the hum of New York's subway, or the rhythmic beep of a hospital ward's monitors.

Curiosity defies the world's obsession with certainty. It keeps life alive, connects you to others, and reminds you that your corner isn't the whole map.

Looking back, I think it was always there. A constant I didn't have a name for. In childhood, it made me read far beyond my age and challenge teachers with unanswerable questions. In nursing, it kept me lingering after shifts to watch procedures I wasn't assigned to. I thought it was restlessness or ambition in disguise, but it was the same impulse pulling at me across decades. An insistent need to understand the moving parts of the world and my place in it.

Eureka moments — some changed my life, some my mind.

But the one I return to most is this: *my life won't follow a straight line.* It will be a constellation. A collection of moments, roles, and identities that may not make sense at first, but eventually form a picture worth seeing.

I once underlined a line in Paulo Coelho's *The Alchemist*:

> *"When you want something,*
> *all the universe conspires in helping you to achieve it."*

I didn't fully understand it then. Now, I do — not as magic, but as momentum. Not as fate, but as faith.

When you move toward something with honesty — a calling, a curiosity, a version of yourself you haven't fully met yet — the world tilts slightly to meet you. But only if you're paying attention. Only if you keep going.

Curiosity is how I pay attention. It's what kept me from giving up when I failed the NCLEX. It's what brought me back to the legal world after years in scrubs. It's what pushed me to launch my own practice when there was no roadmap. Dreams sometimes just whisper. You must be curious enough to lean in and listen.

Eureka moments didn't just give me answers; they kept changing the questions. They turned a comma-hunting lawyer into a dealmaker, a floor-sprinting nurse into someone who could stand still without guilt, a migrant into a man who could call more than one place home. Each was less about the exclamation point and more about the edit. A shift that made the sentence of my life read differently. That's how they shaped me — not in one dramatic scene, but in a thousand small rewrites.

I've never claimed to have all the answers. But I have learned how to ask better questions. And to stay willing. To stay open, to start again, to believe that life isn't just for survival but for examination and rerouting. That's how we find our treasures: *ourselves*.

Eureka isn't a destination. It's a kind of seeing. And I hope I never stop looking.

—

I hadn't become someone new. I'd become someone true.

And truth doesn't always arrive with applause, but with weight. With wind. With resistance. To live in alignment is to stand exposed, upright, sometimes alone. That's cost of clarity. Once you've seen who you are, you can't keep bending to fit what you're not. So, the next lesson wasn't about forward motion. It was about grounded stillness. About spine. About learning — gently, fiercely — the art of standing upright in the wind.

—

But even after clarity, in dreams, a different life tries to visit. One that wears my face, but not my soul.

Soul Notes

❖ What belief have you recently outgrown and what truth took its place?

❖ Where are you waiting for permission, when all you need is courage?

❖ When was the last time you saw something familiar and finally understood it differently?

Interlude: The Life I Almost Lived

"All that is gold does not glitter. Not all those who wander are lost. The old that is strong does not wither. Deep roots are not reached by the frost."
— J.R.R. Tolkien

In my final year at Magpet National High School, emissaries from the capital arrived bearing news that shimmered with improbable promise. A 25% scholarship for top students to study law at Ateneo de Manila University. To the others, it was an announcement. To me, it was a summons.

I believed in destiny then. Not the divine kind, but the kind etched into brochures and sealed in brown envelopes. The kind that came with embossed letterheads and smelled faintly of old paper and new possibilities.

I pleaded with Nanay. She held the brochure, lips moving in silent calculation. Even with the discount, the cost was still impossible. Tuition, yes, but also the price of entering a world never meant for us. Some children inherit scholarships before they learn to spell. Others inherit ceilings.

She said no. I asked again. And Nanay, who bent for others but rarely for herself, bent for me.

—

Ateneo was another country. Law wasn't about justice there. It was about cadence, polish, lineage. My classmates wore linen and ease. I wore second-hand ambition sewn with invisible thread. They spoke of ski trips and silent auctions. I spoke of study schedules and prayer. Not because I lacked imagination, but because leisure was a language I hadn't yet learned.

I smiled when I didn't understand. I laughed when I wasn't in on the joke. I stopped inviting Nanay to visit. Her clothes would've told the truth her words tried to hide — they weren't bought in any store the rich named aloud.

To stay enrolled, I mortgaged her future. Took out loans under her name. Each signature another thread pulled from our already-thin safety net.

I missed her birthday. Then her surgery. Then everything.

She once left a voicemail — long, unhurried, full of mundane tenderness. She asked if I'd eaten. Told me to wear socks while studying. I never called back.

After she died, I found a shoebox in her closet. Inside, every medal I'd ever won. Even the ones they gave just for showing up.

—

I returned to Gubatan once after law school. I couldn't bring myself to walk through the front gate. I told the tricycle driver to keep the meter running. I left a bag of groceries at the doorstep and told myself that was love.

—

Then came Isadora. She was everything I wasn't. The daughter of dynasty, shaped in the symmetry of privilege. Her family didn't open doors. They held the keys to the building. Her mother, though never elected, was a cartographer of power. Lines shifted when she nodded.

They called it *'facilitation.'* I called it fascinating.

Isadora once cried watching an OFW documentary on TV, then, in the next breath, reminded our driver to iron the seat covers. She wept for struggle in theory. In practice, she outsourced it.

She saw potential in me. I saw a shortcut in her.
She offered me a path paved in power. I took it.

We married. I ascended. Not into love, but into orbit, where money softened consequence, politeness passed for principle, and acquiescence masqueraded as public service. I smiled in photos. I studied the script. I played the part, even when the mirror wouldn't return my gaze.

—

I never studied nursing. Never cleaned a wound. Never begged an embassy staffer to expedite my visa. My passport was filled with stamps but empty of story.

I had bodyguards. Assistants. Helpers who called me *'Sir'* even when I forgot their names. I didn't line up. I didn't kneel. I didn't weep on borrowed pillows. I simply arrived where others bled to get.

Her mother gave me a seat at the firm. *"On paper only, so you can focus on politics."*

I ran for Mayor. I promised roads. I redirected funds. I became fluent in ribbon-cuttings. They clapped. Some even cried. Their sons were in Dubai, breaking their backs to send rice money home. I was already home, and they thought that meant something.

But I had learned the choreography. Attend the wake. Cut the ribbon. Smile for the photo. Say *'service'* in English, *'utang na loob'* in Tagalog, and mean neither.

—

What we called public service was really pageantry. A theatre of help that never threatened the script.

I didn't disrupt the system. I inherited it.

I became the kind of man who tweets gratitude to nurses but never tips them. Who praises resilience while building walls to keep it out. Who says *"We must do better"* without ever meaning to.

—

And then, one night, at a scholarship gala I barely remembered agreeing to attend, I met someone. He was Filipino, but not of my kind. His vowels curved softly, as if worn down by time abroad. He spoke of visas and vessels, of arriving and not belonging. Of mothers who prayed for sons with empty pockets and brave hearts.

He said: *"Some of us leave not because we want to, but because we weren't born with the luxury to stay."*

The audience clapped. I didn't. Because I knew him.
Or — I almost did.

He was the version of me who left. Who *zigzagged.* Who folded blankets in hospital wards, and stood in embassies clutching printed dreams. Who loved his mother enough to disappoint her slowly, but never disappeared entirely.

—

I woke up in silk sheets. Married to a woman I could no longer recognize. In a house with too many walls and no welcome. Her presence erased me gently. The kind of absence that passes for safety if you don't look too closely. We weren't at war. We were in costume. We just performed the perfect tableau of power. But inside, I knew. Freedom was a language I never learned to speak aloud.

There was no applause. Just the low hum of the air conditioner.

I rolled over. Checked my phone. Meetings. Mergers. Invitations to cut ribbons. No one needed me. They just needed my signature.

—

This is the life I almost lived. The one where I stayed. Where I succeeded. In metrics I can no longer respect. In that life, I became everything I was told to admire. And nothing I could love. The system didn't change me. It revealed me.

This version of me never left. But he never arrived either.

He hovered — an echo of who I might have been.

—

Author's Note: This interlude is a fictionalized alternate life created for literary and thematic purposes. Any resemblance to real persons, living or dead, is purely coincidental.

Chapter 25: The Art of Standing Upright in the Wind

I used to carry crops on my back down the hills of Pangao-an. The slope was steep, the air thick with the scent of wet earth and sun-baked grass. Each step pressed grit into my soles, each shift of the bamboo basket left a damp groove in my shoulders. And yet, despite the constant shifting, the essence of who I am has always followed me.

I didn't call it resilience back then. It was just life. The muscle memory of children who learn early that standing upright is not just about posture, but about persistence.

The wind at the top of the hill was fierce and unfiltered, tugging at my shirt, daring me to bend. I didn't. I wasn't fearless, but I had no choice. You learn balance when your load is heavy and the ground is uneven. You learn uprightness when the alternative is to fall.

We are often carried by the wind, the unseen current nudging us toward choices, directions, destinies we don't always fully understand. It stirs when you begin to take shape. When your voice grows steadier, your posture more certain, when you dare to want beyond what's permitted.

It always unmistakable. A subtle pressure that arrives the moment you stop shrinking to fit. It carries the weight of memory, expectation, inheritance to ask if you will lean or stand.

—

The biggest turning points in life rarely arrive with fanfare. They don't wait for the world's greenlight. More often, they come in the stillness after striving, when the noise dies down and all you can hear is the voice you've been silencing for years. It's in that moment you realize how long you've spent editing yourself. And for the first time, you're finally ready to publish.

I thought I'd feel different when I passed the New York Bar Exam.
Or when I passed the NCLEX.
Or when I founded ONOR Immigration Law.

I thought I finally found him — a man fully emerged.

But what I felt wasn't celebration. It was silence. The kind that echoes because someone is missing.

My Nanay wasn't there. Not in the way I wanted her to be. Alive, proud, fussing over what I wore to court, or asking if I remembered to eat. She saw the study sessions, the exhaustion, the sacrifices. But not the moment they bloomed. Not the versions of me she quietly raised. Nurse, lawyer, writer, speaker, son. Not the joy that finally caught up to the grind.

But even that list wasn't complete. Some versions of me never made it into the introductions. Shaped in silence, carried in private, shared only in glimpses. I've known what it is to hold tenderness. To long for softness in places built for strength. To follow paths that had no name at the time, only direction. And to walk them anyway.

This isn't a declaration so much as a recognition. That the courage I've tried to live with — in different countries and in different selves — must include this too. That becoming yourself isn't about performance. It's about return. And return, ultimately, means coming home to all of it.

She was gone before I thought I finally arrived.
And yet, in some way, she *is* here.
Not in the ovations, but in the silence that follows.

Because I didn't build this for me alone. I built it for the version of me she believed in before I ever saw him. For the child she raised to be diligent, but who, somewhere along the way, also learned to be daring. For the spirit she carried in sacrifice. The migrant kind, the kind that moves without complaint, works without thanks, loves without limits.

I carry that now. Not because I know how. But because I *must.*

—

For a long time, I confused invisibility with safety, as if blending in was some kind of shield. I thought fitting in meant folding myself smaller. Neat corners, neutral tones, polite nods, and a disappearing act dressed as humility. It was easier to become a silhouette than risk being the painting.

But even silhouettes get tired of standing in someone else's light. They long for edges, color, contour. The full shape of a life no longer dimmed.

The turning point wasn't a thunderclap. It was subtle shift. The first time I looked in the mirror and thought, *What if I stopped editing myself?* A blazer became more than fabric. It was punctuation in a sentence I was finally ready to write. A cologne wasn't just a scent, but a signature. Style became my way of telling the truth without saying a word. About who I was, who I'd been, and who I refused to hide anymore.

Hence, I began showing up in the world just a little more... *vivid.* Not to perform. Not to provoke. But to be seen — fully, finally — for my strength of character, my contribution, and my humanity. A nurse, a lawyer, a friend, a brother, but above all, a person. As a human being.

—

And yet, in invisibility, there's a new kind of erasure. One that praises you with surprise. I've noticed a pattern. The more articulate you are as a brown migrant, the more likely people are to treat it as a fluke.

When I shared this memoir to early readers, a few have called the writing *'polished'*, as if polish were a surprise. As if clarity, rhythm, or reflection required a particular pedigree.

I've learned to hear these comments for what they often are. Not critiques of craft, but collisions with expectation. When a white man with an MFA writes lyrically, it's called literary. When someone like me — a Filipino nurse, lawyer, migrant — does the same, it's unexpected. As if all the credentials, EQ, grit, and lived experience were just a lucky glitch in the algorithm.

But these words weren't shaped in a writer's residency. They were written in the pauses. Between call bells and case files, visa queues and midnight shifts.

The polish isn't performance. It's practice. And the voice isn't borrowed. It's built. Slowly, across continents, from the cadence of stories I had to live before I could ever write them down.

So, if the prose feels unexpected, it's not the polish that's unfamiliar.

It's who's holding the pen.

It's time the world adjusted its idea of what excellence can look and sound like.

—

@thestylishasianman — my Instagram handle, yes, but also my manifesto. A declaration that being a man of substance and meaning isn't at odds with being well-dressed. It is my badge of honor, my resistance, my ode to the heritage stitched into my name and my bones. He didn't arrive with swagger, but with intention. Not as an alter ego, but as a reclamation. Of space. Of voice. Of joy.

A soft rebellion wrapped in sharp tailoring. It wasn't about vanity, but visibility. About choosing not to vanish. About taking up space without asking first. About walking into the world and saying, *"Here I am"*.

Style is never just about fabric. It's about truth-telling in silk and cotton, about choosing the cut that suits your convictions. Like the time I walked into my first client meeting wearing a bold navy pinstripe, not to impress, but because it felt like me. That suit didn't win the case, but it reminded me I belonged in the room.

Style, at its best, is the testimony of the courage to match the outside to the inside. And when I did embrace myself, people noticed. Some smiled. Some stared. Some didn't know what to make of it. But I had never felt more like myself.

Of course, not everyone applauds when you stop apologizing. But I've learned that discomfort in others is not a reason to disappear. If anything, it's a reason to shine brighter, like a lighthouse that makes no apologies for where it stands.

Humor helped. I told the jokes (even the bad ones, and oh, there were many) because laughter disarms. It tells people, *"I'm not a threat."* I'm just a man who knows that matching socks with a pocket square doesn't mean I'm not serious about life. It just means I enjoy it.

There's a dignity in ease. In knowing who you are and letting the world adjust. Not the other way around. I no longer audition for spaces. I curate them.

And yet, the wind still blows.

Some mornings, the wind arrives as *hesitation*. There were moments — casual conversations, new rooms, unfamiliar eyes — when I paused just a breath too long before speaking. I often had the words, but I would question whether I had the right to say them. Whether I belonged at all. And yet, I straightened my spine, cleared my throat, and spoke anyway. Because standing upright isn't about silencing the wind. It's about hearing it — and rising, still.

Other days, the wind disguises itself as *doubt*. A whisper asking if I should fold myself smaller. If the world prefers the softer version. But then I catch my reflection — the shoes, the stance, the smirk — and I remember: *muted was never me.*

Now I dress for the person I've become. To express myself. I wear color on grey days. I wear pride in the posture. I wear history in the hemline. I walk into rooms with all of me. Unbuttoned just enough to let the heart show.

Because when the world tries to iron you flat, the boldest resistance is to remain unmistakably textured. To keep your wrinkles and wear them like embroidery. Not mistakes to be hidden, but flourishes of your becoming. Not imperfections to iron out, but reminders of where you've stretched, softened, survived.

There's a kind of elegance in effort made visible. What Italians call *sprezzatura* — the art of effortlessness that comes only from having earned every crease. Imperfect, but present. That ease that's only earned after you've worn life well.

—

Standing upright in the wind doesn't shout. It is an art, but it doesn't arrive with confetti or declarations. It slips in like a friend at dusk, carrying something honest but unspoken. Just a story stitched from softer threads.

A story about the triumph of showing up as yourself. Inch by inch. About learning to stand or walk into a room without shrinking. To let your difference sit beside you, not something to be hidden behind pleasantries and pleats.

It's about making peace with all the selves we carry — the bold, the bashful, the still-emerging.

If you've ever folded yourself to fit, reshaped your laughter to sound more polite, dimmed your color to match someone else's palette —

If you've ever stood in front of a mirror wondering or rehearsing how much to reveal —

I hope you find a sliver of yourself here.

Not just in the clothes, but in the courage. In the softness. In the steady resolve.

—

I used to carry crops on my back. Now, I carry legacy. Same spine, different load.

The soil taught me discipline. The sweat taught me reverence. I didn't know then that those long walks were training me to carry something far heavier. And far less visible: *legacy*.

I used to think building a legacy meant being fearless. Like standing tall on a stage, chin up, back straight, with all your doubts neatly ironed out. But now I know, legacy is the joy of continuing even when the ones who loved you first aren't there to see it.

I miss Nanay every day. But when I slip on a blazer with a pop of color, when I help a client, when I nurse a patient, when I write 'Founder' under my name, she's there. Not as a ghost, but as a grin. As the warmth in my chest. As the voice that says, *"Carry on. With style."*

Because this now goes beyond work, it is about how I dance with grief, how I thread joy through legacy, and how I build something not in spite of loss, but because of love.

It's a thank-you note. A flag in the ground. A little bit Filipino, a little bit fabulous. It's the best of what I've been given, turned outward.

—

This life — my *noble and honorable adventure* — sacred, zigzagged, stitched with plane tickets and prayers — has never moved in straight lines. But that's the beauty of it.

I've fumbled and flown, grieved and grown, crossed oceans with nothing but a passport and a prayer. But I've come to understand that the life's unfolding isn't a destination. It's a rhythm you keep. A vow you renew. A story you dare to keep writing even when the ink runs low.

That's the most noble and honorable adventure of all —
not the world we conquer, but the self we come home to.

So here I am — not a finished product, but a well-worn map.
Creased by detours. Inked with becoming. I'm still learning, still
laughing. Still stepping into rooms like they're already mine.

A little braver in the tailoring. A little gentler in the soul.

With the wind at my back and a vow stitched into every seam:

I will no longer shrink to be palatable.
I will no longer fold to be carried.
I will wear the fullness of who I am.

—

These days, I walk upright in the wind.
With color in my collar and courage in my spine.

The wind doesn't stop. But I no longer flinch.
Or I try my best not to.

Nursing. Law. Love. Legacy.

This work, this life — it's my offering.

To her.
To home.
To anyone who's ever wondered if dreaming was allowed.

Because the boldest outfit I've ever worn is the truth —
and the life I'll ever live is the one where I refuse to disappear.

And if you're standing at the threshold of your own truth —
may it be the boldest thing you dare to wear.

Soul Notes

❖ What would it look like to dress, not just for the day ahead but for the life you're meant to live?

❖ What part of you have you kept safely tucked away and what might unfold if you let it step into the light?

❖ Which version of you is still waiting to be expressed?

Epilogue: Your Noble and Honorable Adventure

When I first set out to write this memoir, I thought I was charting the story of how I moved through the world. But in making sense of my experiences, I discovered a thread running through every season:

Identity shaping my roots.
Courage moving my feet.
Becoming giving me wings.

So, what ties it all together? A steady pulse.

Identity whispered who I was.
Courage dared me to try anyway.
Becoming reminded me that I am still unfolding.

—

One of the hardest lessons I've had to learn, and relearn, is to trust the strange, winding shape of my own path. Like walking a forest trail without a map, discovering a route only I could walk.

It was during my early nursing days, after a shift that had wrung me out from the inside. A patient had coded. Another wouldn't stop screaming. I hadn't eaten, I'd barely sat down, and I was still trying to prove I belonged in a world engineered to keep people like me on the edge.

I remember walking home, boots soaked and spirit heavier still, after a colleague dismissed me as *'not ICU material.'* The rain was thin but relentless. It trickled past my collar and settled in the bones. My scrubs clung damp against my skin. Streetlights flickered in puddles. The city moved on, indifferent, while I slowed not from exhaustion, but from a deeper sting. I've questioned if I've mistaken this calling for a delusion.

I didn't know it then, but that moment was a reroute. A disruption with its own kind of compass. It was a reminder that even the hardest roads can still lead to a noble and honorable adventure.

For a while, it broke me. I lost my confidence. Nursing was the life I had chosen then, and I made myself believe that I wasn't good enough for it. It was one thing to be told I couldn't start with law. But to be told I had no place in the industry I had slowly embraced? That cut deeper. It made me revisit my instincts, my grit, my worth.

For all its talk of healing, healthcare can be a ruthless place. Behind the compassion are hierarchies, egos, and gatekeepers who decide who deserves to stay. And for a time, I believed them.

But just around the corner, in a bookstore lit like forgiveness, I stumbled upon a copy of *T.E. Oh's Intensive Care Manual* — as if the universe, in its own rebuttal, had already written me back in.

A spark. A signal. An affirmation.

I carried that book through exams and endless shifts. A reminder that I did belong. And years later, I gave it away to someone who needed it more. Because belief, once kindled, becomes even more powerful when shared.

Doubt, that slick little shape-shifter, showed up in every chapter, sometimes dressed as impostor syndrome, sometimes as logic in a bad outfit. It didn't shout. It whispered: *Who do you think you are?*

But I've learned to whisper back: *Becoming.*

—

When I finished law, I thought the path would be linear. Join
BigLaw, climb the ladder, make partner, and call it a life. A clean
arc. Prestigious. Predictable. But somewhere between European
boardrooms and late-night redlines, I began asking harder
questions.

Is this all there is?
Is this the legacy I'm leaving behind?
Is this the only shape that success can take?

Those questions didn't arrive all at once. They crept in through
ambition's side door. And the more I asked, the clearer it became.
Every chapter — nursing, law, migration — was a design.

I wanted a career, but more so, a compass to guide me toward
purpose. And over time, that clarity took form. In a cross-border
legal practice built not just to elevate my name, but to build
something bigger. A legacy for my family. A bridge for others. A
map that might outlive me.

—

We spend much of our lives looking sideways. Comparing,
competing, checking how far ahead or behind we are on someone
else's invisible timeline sketched in disappearing ink. But life is not
a race. It's a narrative. And you are the author.

We're sold this myth that success arrives on schedule — clean,
certain, applauded. As if life hands out medals for punctuality. But
value isn't something someone else bestows. It's something you
decide to carry, especially when it feels too heavy.
Becoming is not a checklist. And timing is personal.

The journey is not linear. Sometimes it sidesteps, stumbles, then sways into joy like a rhythm only you were meant to follow. There is dignity in every chapter. Not because we always choose wisely or win greatly, but because we dare.

Dare to question.
To want more.
To laugh out loud.
To stay.

That's the revolution:

Becoming isn't about arriving.
It's about unlearning the need to.

The road doesn't have to be straight.
It just has to be honest.

Even detours can be noble.
Even wanderers can be honorable.

It's the slow act of unbecoming who the world told you to be. And slowly returning to the shape of your own soul.

—

I used to think growing up meant getting it right. Turns out, I'm still gloriously naïve. Just in more intentional ways. I still follow the voice inside me, even when it stutters. Especially when it stutters.

For every shift I worked, every visa I chased, every exam I sat, and every solo walk I took through a foreign city, curiosity was the thread that kept pulling me forward. A desire to understand the world, and in doing so, understand myself.

It took me years, countries, careers, and whole seasons of doubt to realize I was allowed to write a story that didn't impress everyone, so long as it's mine.

I used to think I was running toward a destination. But I was turning into a *flâneur* — a wanderer who moves not to escape, but to witness. Not from above, but from within. Someone who stops for the wildflowers and still makes it to the gate on time, even if it's the wrong terminal.

Because the point was never to impress everyone, but to become someone your younger self might recognize. The kind who dares not just to dream, but to remain.

We realize that wandering isn't a delay but a discipline.
That what feels like aimlessness is often wisdom in disguise.

Which brings me to *Hadestown* —
a myth retold as a musical about love, doubt, and daring to sing the truth even when the world doesn't believe in you.

Orpheus doesn't fight with a sword. He walks through the underworld armed only with a song. Love is fragile, but still worth trying for, even if the ending isn't guaranteed.

We carry two stories: the life we have and the life we hope for.
And sometimes, rewriting the ending starts with believing you deserve one.

The journey isn't just about closing the gap.
It's about choosing which story to fight for and how to keep singing, even when your voice shakes.

So don't just pass through life.
Venture. Risk. Begin again.

Novie Onor

Let your story be sewn not just with resilience, but with intention.
Choose paths that make your spirit stand taller.
Seek adventures that test your mettle and reveal your tenderness.

When the world tells you to shrink, to wait, to earn your place,
let identity be your compass and courage your fuel.

Move with restrained nobility. With unshakable honor.
Not because you are certain, but because you are taking shape.

Let your life be adventurous.
Let it be noble.
Let it be honorable.

In how you stay curious.
In how you remain alive.

—

When I look back on my life, I'm proud of the places I've reached,
the borders I've crossed, the careers I've built across continents.
But all those accomplishments, impressive as they may look on a
résumé, pale in comparison to the things that mattered:

Finding inner peace.
Knowing who you are.
Working on your life's meaning.

And offering yourself — fully —
to your family, your community, and your corner of the world.

I used to think I had to earn my wings to prove myself valuable
before I could take flight. But the wings were never the prize.
They were the reminder that I've always had what I needed to rise.

212

You, too.

You are worthy. In the waiting. In the wandering.

Even — especially — when you're unsure.

Let your life be a map that only you could draw.
Let your milestones be moments of grace.
Let your path be real.

Because even in the wandering, you were already enough.

Your roots don't need to be shed to grow wings —
they're part of the lift.
Just trust the wind beneath both.

Wander, yes — but wander like you mean it.
With your wings on.
With your name intact.

That's the legacy.
That's the revolution.
That's your noble and honorable adventure.

Soul Notes

❖ What kind of life would feel like your own?

❖ What does becoming mean to you and how will you honor that answer, today?

❖ What would your own noble and honorable adventure look like starting now?

Claim and Conquer
(Or: Why This Book Is a Mirror)

As you reach this final page, I want to hand you the pen.

This was never just a memoir. It was always a mirror.

If something stirred in you — a memory, a restlessness, a half-buried dream — don't shove it aside. Listen.

That's a signal. That's you, waking up.

This book was written to say *you can go too.*
In your way, on your terms, with your own rhythm and grit.

When I first read *The Year of Magical Thinking, On Earth We're Briefly Gorgeous, Educated,* and *I Know Why the Caged Bird Sings,* I read them breathlessly. I wanted to write like them. But I couldn't, so I wrote like me. With a legal mind, a nurse's hands, a migrant's memory, and a storyteller's voice.

Not polished. Not tidy. But always real. And fully mine.

I once admired those who walked with certainty. Mentors who lit the way. But I learned that you can't borrow someone else's map. You draw your own by walking it.

Perhaps that's your next chapter.
Perhaps your own *noble and honorable adventure* begins like this:
- Saying yes to what scares you
- Saying no to what no longer fits
- Reclaiming the part of you that's been waiting to breathe

Not a perfect plan. Just one honest step.

The path won't be linear.
But it will be yours.

So perhaps this is your moment to *claim and conquer*.

And if the mirror is honest, it will show you that the arena is waiting.

I take my cue from Theodore Roosevelt's *Man in the Arena*, first delivered at the Sorbonne — the same halls where I once studied, walked past stone archways, and learned that courage is a practice. But my arenas have never been just one place. They've been spaces where the rules weren't written for me, so I learned to write my own.

The credit will never belong to the critic who stayed safe in the gallery. It belongs to the one who dares. Who claims their seat when none is offered, who risks the sting of failure for the taste of victory, who stands where the blows land and still leans forward. You do not wait to be chosen. You choose yourself. You step in, stand tall, and conquer. The arena does not reward the timid. It remembers the brave.

Claim your voice. Conquer gently.

Move forward with courage.
Let kindness be your shield.
Let willpower be your sword.

Because *Noble and Honorable Adventures* doesn't end here.
It lives on as a community and a space where courage is shared.

Where identity is respected.
Where nuance is welcome.
Where we dare to keep becoming together.

If you'd like to keep walking together — through ideas, stories, immigration journeys, cross-cultural stories, or simply real conversation — I'm here. You're welcome.

Don't wait.
Travel true.
Begin where you are.

May your next chapter be wild, worthy, and wholly your own.

PS: I read every message. If this book stirred something in you, I'd love to hear what your mirror revealed. Let's keep the conversation going —
novie@onoradvisory.com | novie@onorimmigrationlaw.com

GLOSSARY

of UNCOMMON AND FOREIGN WORDS

and CULTURAL REFERENCES

Abel Tasman *(New Zealand)* – A coastal track in the south island of New Zealand. Referenced as the trail of beauty, bruises, and badly timed footwear.

Acropolis *(Greece)* – Ancient citadel in Athens containing the Parthenon. Referenced as a place that makes you feel like a comma in the sentence of history.

Adobo *(Philippines)* – A national dish made with soy sauce, vinegar, garlic, and bay leaves. Referenced as home and memory in edible form.

AHPRA *(Australia)* – Australian Health Practitioner Regulation Agency. Oversees nursing registration in the author's professional journey.

Alcatraz *(United States)* – A former prison on an island in San Francisco Bay.

Alhambra *(Spain)* – A palace and fortress complex in Granada, Spain. Referenced to convey beauty, history, and the layered complexity of place.

Allez! *(France)* – "Go!" Often heard courtside at Roland Garros and in other sports stadiums. Used to capture emotional surge, urgency, and an international rallying spirit.

Anak *(Philippines)* – Tagalog term of endearment meaning "my child." Reflects the warmth of Filipino familial language, often exchanged between the author and his elders.

Andalusia *(Spain)* – A region in southern Spain known for its Moorish architecture and flamenco. Referenced as a romanticized backdrop to wandering.

Anne *(Proper name)* – The friend who introduced the author to ICU. A pivotal figure who opened a doorway into a new chapter of the author's professional life.

Antokolsky, Pavel *(Proper name)* – Soviet poet known for works on grief and endurance. Referenced to reflect emotional resonance with loss.

Aotearoa *(Māori)* – The Māori name for New Zealand, meaning "Land of the Long White Cloud." Referenced as promise, home, and spiritual compass.

Apfelschorle *(Germany)* – Drink made from sparkling water and apple juice. Common refreshment in German chapters.

Archimedes *(Proper name)* – An ancient Greek mathematician and inventor. Referenced to symbolize intellectual awakening and curious spirit.

Aspiras, Miko *(Proper name)* – An acclaimed Filipino pastry chef celebrated for his innovative desserts and modern approach to traditional Filipino flavors. Internationally recognized for his artistry and a leading voice in the Philippines' culinary scene.

Astronomical Clock *(Czech Republic)* – A medieval clock in Prague known for its hourly show of moving figures. Serves as a metaphor for spectacle, brevity, and meaning-making.

Ate *(Philippines)* – A respectful term for an older sister or female figure. Common in Filipino culture and the author's upbringing. Represents hierarchy, care, and cultural intimacy.

Ateneo de Manila University *(Philippines)* – A prestigious Jesuit university in the Philippines. Referenced to contextualize educational privilege and power structures.

Auf geht's! *(Germany)* – "Let's get moving!" German rallying spirit.

Aurelius, Marcus *(Proper name)* – An ancient Roman emperor and philosopher king, author of *Meditations*. Referenced as a guiding voice during moments of internal reckoning and a reminder that leadership begins with self.

Auntie Belen *(Proper name)* – Referenced both personally and culturally as the archetype of a hardworking OFW nurse.

Aurora Australis *(Natural Phenomenon)* – The Southern Lights. A cousin to the more famous Aurora Borealis, but quieter and more elusive. Referenced as a metaphor for guidance through mystery.

Baon *(Philippines)* – Filipino term for food or allowance brought to school or work, symbolizing family care and frugality. A cultural gesture of care used as shorthand for sacrifice, preparation, and motherly love.

Bach, Johann Sebastian *(Proper name)* – German classical composer whose music represents stillness, reverence, and emotional universality. Mentioned by the author in moments of cultural immersion.

Baklava *(Middle East/Greece)* – A pastry of filo, nuts, and syrup.

Balikbayan *(Philippines)* – A returning Filipino citizen or OFW. Also refers to the large boxes filled with goods to show love from afar and economic diaspora.

Barangay *(Philippines)* – The smallest administrative unit in the Philippines, like a village or neighborhood. Forms the backdrop of the author's early life in Mindanao. Represents hyper-local identity and governance.

Barangay midwife *(Philippines)* – A community health worker who assists with childbirth and basic care in rural areas. Mentioned in connection with the birth of the author and early memories of grassroots healthcare.

Bayaran taka ugma, promise *(Philippines)* – Cebuano for "I'll pay you tomorrow, promise." A tongue-in-cheek phrase that reflects local humor and informal credit systems.

Becoming *(United States)* – Memoir by Michelle Obama. Referenced as a touchstone text during reflections on identity, ambition, and leadership.

Bienveillance *(France)* – Means "kindness" or "benevolence." Referenced as a value encountered during French legal studies and cultural immersion.

BigLaw *(Global)* – Slang for elite corporate law firms known for long hours and prestige. Referenced when choosing meaning over the high-performance legal world.

Bilbao *(Spain)* – A city in northern Spain known for the Guggenheim Museum and its mix of industrial history and modern architecture.

Bitcoin *(Global)* – A digital currency created and held electronically, without a central bank. Symbol of modern finance and speculative risk.

Blackstone *(Legal)* – Refers to Sir William Blackstone, an English jurist whose Commentaries on the Laws of England became foundational in legal education. Mentioned to show legal tradition and the kind of textbooks that come with a moral hangover.

Boba *(Taiwan/United Staes)* – A drink with tapioca pearls, popular in Asian communities worldwide. Referenced during a cultural exploration in Sydney, symbolizing diasporic joy.

Bond villain *(Fictional)* – The classic over-the-top antagonist from James Bond films with all dramatic monologues, secret lairs, and global domination plots.

Bonjour *(France)* – "Good day." More than a greeting in France, it's a social expectation and conversation opener. The author learns the importance of this ritual in Paris, where even bakery interactions begin with it. Forget it, and you'll be met with silence.

Boulangerie *(France)* – A bakery specializing in bread and viennoiseries. Symbol of daily ritual in French life. Evoked in the Paris chapter as part of daily routine and culinary ritual.

Bourdain, Anthony *(Proper name)* – American chef, writer, and travel documentarian. Known for exploring food as cultural bridge. Quoted as inspiration for movement and later echoed in the chapter's close as a philosophy of connection.

Brahms, Johannes *(Proper name)* – Austrian-German Romantic composer known for his depth and brooding brilliance and a fixture of Vienna's musical heritage. Evoked as the soundtrack of introspection.

Brahmsstraße *(Germany)* – A residential street in Germany named after composer Johannes Brahms. Referenced during a Sydney Symphony performance, it becomes a symbol of how past lives echo in present moments and where music, memory, and movement intersect.

Bratwurst *(Germany)* – German sausage made from pork, beef, or veal.

Brisbane Convention Centre *(Australia)* – A sleek riverside venue in South Bank, known for hosting graduations, conferences, and once, the author's silent moment of clarity. Referenced as the physical backdrop to an internal milestone and the pivot point between survival and becoming.

Brisbane River *(Australia)* – The winding river that flows through the heart of Brisbane, calm and unhurried. Referenced as metaphor where time flowed gently and the author realized that law was a delayed beginning.

Bronte *(Australia)* – A beachside suburb in Sydney. Referenced as a site of reflection and coastal grounding.

Bronze Age *(Global/Historical)* – Prehistoric era marked by metallurgy and early civilization. Referenced metaphorically to frame human instinct for movement and meaning.

Buffalo Convention Center *(United States)* – The frozen coliseum where New York Bar Exam dreams go to sweat, panic, and rehydrate with gas station coffee.

Bulad *(Philippines)* – Dried, salted fish. Often fried and eaten with rice and vinegar. A humble, potent flavor of home. A recurring symbol of home, hunger, and humble beginnings. Its sharp, proud, and persistent smell lingers in the memory.

Bulalo *(Philippines)* – A slow-cooked beef marrow stew from the Philippines. Symbolically tied to comfort, warmth, and cultural grounding.

Burger King *(Global)* – An international fast-food chain known for its flame-grilled burgers, particularly the Whopper.

Burleigh Heads *(Australia)* – The author's weekend escape during the Queensland chapter. Sun, surf, and a moment to breathe.

Café Central *(Austria)* – A grand old café in Vienna once frequented by Freud, Trotsky, and future revolutions. Chandeliers, marble columns, and conspiracies over cake. A place where ideas steeped longer than tea.

Caipirinha *(Brazil)* – Brazil's national cocktail made with cachaça, lime, and sugar.

Camus, Albert *(Proper name)* – Philosopher of the absurd and author of *The Stranger*. Referenced as literary company during periods of reflection and existential fatigue.

Carmel *(Proper name)* – Fellow nurse, trusted friend, and unexpected soul sister. Nicknamed *Captain Carmel* not for rank, but for radiance. In a life toggling between hospital shifts and existential spirals, she's proof that friendship can feel like coming home. Irish by passport, universal by presence.

Cassava / Balanghoy *(Philippines)* – A starchy root used in desserts and local dishes. Common in rural meals. Used as a metaphor for resilience.

Castel Sant'Angelo *(Italy)* – A fortress in Rome, used symbolically to represent tourist fatigue and poetic stillness. The author naps on a monobloc chair here, capturing the absurd exhaustion of solo travel, and the poetry found in everyday pauses.

Catcher in the Rye *(United States)* – Novel by J.D. Salinger. Referenced for shaping early views on authenticity and resistance to pretense.

Caulfield, Holden *(Fictional)* – Protagonist of *The Catcher in the Rye*. Referenced in discussions of literary influence and coming-of-age disillusionment.

Cebu *(Philippines)* – A province in the Visayas region of the Philippines. Mentioned as a cultural and regional touchstone. Represents a place of pride and identity for many Filipinos, including those in diaspora.

Cecille *(Proper name)* – A friend who joined an East Coast road trip. Another with the same name mentioned as a single mother and lawyer who built a life of ambition and service and referenced as a force of grit and grace.

Chaka Khan *(Proper name)* – Global Queen of Funk. American Grammy-winning powerhouse whose voice can lift moods, melt resistance, and summon courage. Referenced as both anthem and attitude for when survival needs a soundtrack and joy had to be loud.

Chanel No. 5 *(France)* – Iconic French perfume created in 1921. Symbol of timeless elegance.

Charles Bridge *(Czech Republic)* – A Gothic stone bridge in Prague adorned with statues. Referenced as a place where art, sound, and presence collided.

Chiaroscuro *(Italy)* – An art technique using strong contrasts between light and dark. Appears in discussions of beauty and perspective.

Chicken Joy *(Philippines)* – The signature fried chicken meal from Jollibee, it is cultural comfort food. Referenced as a nostalgic symbol of Filipino middle-class aspiration.

Chicken Soup for the Soul *(United States)* – A wildly popular book series from the '90s filled with short, heart-tugging essays about everyday people and the courage of being human. An early education in empathy and in feeling things more deeply than you meant to.

Christ the Redeemer *(Brazil)* – Art deco statue of Jesus overlooking Rio. Referenced as a literal and symbolic high point of the cityscape.

Churrasco *(Brazil)* – Barbecue grilled over open flame, often served rodízio-style. Referenced in Rio as a meal that embodied joy, smoke, and simplicity.

Circular Quay *(Australia)* – Transport hub on Sydney Harbour. Referenced as a locus of movement, migration, and ferry-fueled thoughts.

Cité Internationale Universitaire de Paris *(France)* – Student housing complex in Paris for international scholars. Referenced during chapters set in France as a formative, multicultural living space.

Code Brown *(France)* – Nursing slang for a fecal emergency. Referenced during the author's first hospital shift as a student nurse, where caregiving began not with stethoscopes but with clean-ups, humility, and an unexpectedly sacred thank you.

Coelho, Paulo *(Proper name)* – Brazilian author of The Alchemist. Associated with spiritual journeys and personal legend. Referenced as a literary lens for framing the summer's detour as destiny.

Competence Assessment Programme (CAP) *(New Zealand)* – A bridging course for internationally qualified nurses in New Zealand. It was "part bootcamp, part baptism by fire," where competence met culture shock.

Coogee to Bondi walk *(Australia)* – A 6 km coastal track linking two of Sydney's most famous beaches. Passes Gordons Bay, Clovelly, Bronte, and Tamarama before ending at Bondi. Known for cliffside views, ocean pools, and a mix of locals, tourists, and sunrise joggers.

Copacabana *(Brazil)* – Rio's iconic beach known for samba, soccer, and spectacle. Referenced in Rio chapters as backdrop to food, music, and movement.

Curie, Marie *(Proper name)* – Groundbreaking Polish-French physicist and chemist. Invoked as a figure of immigrant brilliance and determination and someone who pursued excellence far from home and against the odds.

Darling Harbour *(Australia)* – A waterfront precinct pulsing with tourists, tugboats, and the scent of salt and street food. For the author, it was less about the attractions and more about the feeling that life was starting to expand.

Department of Home Affairs *(Australia)* – Government department overseeing immigration, citizenship, and border security.

de Beauvoir, Simone *(Proper name)* – French philosopher and feminist. Quoted in Chapter 3, "One is not born, but rather becomes." Her words become a scaffolding for the memoir's themes of identity and becoming.

Didion, Joan *(Proper name)* – Iconic American memoirist known for her precise emotional restraint. Cited as a literary influence. Didion's spare, sharp, devastating voice shapes the memoir's structure and restraint.

Digestive and Liver Unit *(Philippines)* – The first professional battlefield. Smelled like antiseptic and banana, filled with patient stories and medical monitors. Where competence was forged, one chart and colostomy change at a time.

DOC *(New Zealand)* – Department of Conservation. The Kiwi guardian of nature. Manages the Great Walks, huts, and trails. Revered by trampers, feared by rule-breakers, and referenced as scripture in the New Zealand chapters.

Du bist stark. Du bist schön. Du schaffst das. *(Germany)* – "You are strong. You are beautiful. You can do it." A mantra the author encounters and repeats during his time in Frankfurt. It becomes a gentle but powerful affirmation during emotionally and professionally trying moments.

Durian *(Philippines)* – A tropical fruit with a divisive smell and custard-like texture common in Mindanao. Referenced in descriptions of growing up in the south.

Eala, Alexa *(Proper name)* – A professional tennis player and rising star from the Philippines. The first Filipino to win a junior Grand Slam title and enter the WTA Top 50. Mentioned as a symbol of global Filipino excellence and potential.

East Coast *(United States)* – Eastern seaboard of the United States. Home to several personal and professional chapters.

EB-3 Immigrant Visa Application *(United States)* – A U.S. employment-based visa category. Referenced as the legal path the author pursued to continue his professional journey in America.

Educated *(United States)* – Memoir by Tara Westover about growing up in a survivalist family and pursuing education. Cited as an inspiration in the journey of self-definition and voice.

Eiffel Tower *(France)* – Paris's iconic wrought-iron structure. Mentioned in passing as part of a broader meditation on beauty, cliché, and global markers of wonder.

Empire State Building *(United States)* – Iconic skyscraper in New York City. Referenced as a symbol of ambition, it lights up like the dreams of every immigrant.

Epictetus *(Proper name)* – Born enslaved, became an Ancient Greek Stoic philosopher. Preached that while we can't control events, we can always control our response.

Esperanto *(Global)* – A constructed international auxiliary language. Referenced to symbolize universal connection and idealism.

Esperanza *(Philippines)* – A popular 1990s teleserye starring Judy Ann Santos. Referenced in chapters about pop culture, family bonding, and the emotional tone of growing up Filipino.

Espiritu, Erlinda *(Proper name)* – A trailblazing Filipina lawyer who graduated from Harvard Law. Mentioned as an early symbol of proof that someone from the author's country could rise to global heights. Represents aspiration, intellect, and the legacy of excellence that inspired his own legal journey.

Être est mieux qu'avoir *(France)* – "To be is better than to have." A philosophical thread referenced in the author's Paris reflections, tying back to presence over possession.

Eureka *(Ancient Greece)* – Exclamation attributed to Archimedes meaning "I have found it." Referenced in a moment of clarity and academic breakthrough.

Eurovision *(Europe)* – International song contest. Appears as a moment of cultural joy and continental quirkiness.

EU Blue Card *(Europe)* – Work permit for highly skilled non-EU citizens. Mentioned in passing as a credential hard-won during European career pivot.

Excusez-moi, je suis perdu *(France)* – "Excuse me, I'm lost." Used both literally and metaphorically in the Paris chapter. A phrase used literally in Paris, but which also becomes a metaphor for his broader experience navigating foreign systems, identity, and uncertainty.

Facebook *(Social media)* – A global social networking platform launched in 2004, where users can post updates, photos, and "friend" people. Often used for staying connected, sharing life events, or falling into comment-section rabbit holes.

Fashion Week *(Global)* – Industry event where designers showcase seasonal collections. Referenced as a symbol of style, spectacle, and urban energy.

Favela *(Brazil)* – Informal housing communities often associated with poverty and resilience. Referenced to reflect the contrast of urban inequality witnessed during travels.

Febbie *(Proper name)* – The sister who left for Saudi Arabia so the author could go to school. Referenced as a symbol of selfless migration and sibling love.

Federer, Roger *(Proper name)* – One of the greatest tennis players of all time, known for his elegance, efficiency, and composure. Federer's rivalry with Nadal is used to illustrate contrasting approaches to mastery: elegance vs. effort.

Figlmüller Wollzeile *(Austria)* – A historic schnitzel institution in Vienna, famous for serving veal cutlets the size of umbrellas. A culinary rite of passage. Ordered with pride, eaten with awe, and survived with elastic-waisted pants.

Fika *(Sweden)* – A cultural practice of slowing down with coffee and conversation. Referenced not as a break, but as a way of being. One that teaches you how to sit with others, and with yourself.

Fiordland *(New Zealand)* – A rugged region in New Zealand known for dramatic landscapes. Referenced as a site of both physical exhaustion and awe.

Flâneur *(France)* – A contemplative urban stroller or observer. Symbolic of the author's philosophical wandering through cities like Paris and Prague. The flâneur walks not to escape, but to see.

Flat white *(Australia/New Zealand)* – A coffee drink made with espresso and steamed milk. A mainstay of the author's Sydney routine. Represents ritual, grounding, and the small comforts that stitch life together.

Forza! *(Italy)* – "Strength!" or "Let's go!" A cheer used in sports and life. Another international cheer featured in Chapter 9's multilingual montage of resilience.

Foxton *(New Zealand)* – A small town on the lower west coast of New Zealand's North Island, known for its Dutch windmill, flax history, and quiet charm. Referenced as a place of introspection and transition.

Freud, Sigmund *(Proper name)* – Austrian legendary figure regarded as the father of psychoanalysis. Referenced as both an intellectual figure and a cultural backdrop in Vienna.

Fromagerie *(France)* – A cheese shop. Part of the author's immersion in French food culture. Fromageries are as much about art as sustenance, they are a metaphor for choosing beauty even in constraint.

Game of Thrones *(Global)* – HBO fantasy series based on George R.R. Martin's novels. Dubrovnik served as King's Landing. Referenced during a fandom-fueled visit to Croatia turned spiritual solo reset.

Ganbatte! *(Japan)* – "Do your best!" or "Hang in there!" Commonly used as encouragement. One of several international rallying cries the author collects in Chapter 9 (*Vamos*).

Gaudí, Antoni *(Proper name)* – The visionary Catalan architect behind Barcelona's surreal, sinuous landmarks. His work, all curves, color, and spiritual ambition, is less about logic and more about longing. Appears as a symbol of faith made tangible.

Genau *(Germany)* – "Exactly." A catch-all agreement word, used affectionately. Commonly heard in Frankfurt. In the memoir, it becomes a comforting linguistic tic that says, "You're on the right track."

Giegie *(Philippines)* – The author's older sister, described as boyish, brave, and brilliant with horses and humor. Referenced in both childhood adventures and funeral rituals, where she became the family's comic diplomat.

Goethe, Johann Wolfgang von *(Proper name)* – Germany's Shakespeare-meets-soul-searcher. Mentioned when aiming for poetic fluency or just trying not to butcher German grammar.

GoFundMe *(Global)* – Online crowdfunding platform for personal and charitable causes.

Gold Coast University Hospital *(Australia)* – A major public hospital in Queensland, known for its modern design and proximity to the beach. It was the author's first hospital job in Australia — sterile, shiny, and full of unknown buttons. A beginning point for reassembly.

Golden Gate Bridge *(United States)* – A suspension bridge in San Francisco, often cloaked in fog. Referenced as a symbol of crossing over from fear to freedom.

Google *(Global)* – The world's dominant search engine, digital oracle, and accidental therapist. Referenced as the go-to for everything from medication side effects to "how to sound confident when you're scared."

Gubatan *(Philippines)* – A barangay in Magpet, Cotabato. The author's childhood home and his geographic and emotional starting point.

GrabFood *(Southeast Asia)* – Food delivery service. Referenced as a luxury absent from early immigrant life, when dinner meant canned tuna and crackers, not curry in 15 minutes.

Grand Canyon *(United States)* – National park in Arizona referenced as an encounter with the sublime.

Grylls, Bear *(Proper name)* – British survivalist referenced during the author's most harrowing ICU shifts.

Guten Morgen Sonnenschein *(Germany)* – "Good morning, sunshine." Referenced as a phrase that juxtaposed mood and morning ritual.

Hadestown *(United States)* – A Broadway musical based on the myth of Orpheus and Eurydice. Referenced as a creative and emotional landmark. A reminder that fate can be rewritten and art can carry defiance.

Half Dome *(United States)* – A granite beast in Yosemite the author visited it in the U.S. leg of his sabbatical.

Halley's Comet *(Global/Folklore)* – Astronomical event often seen as an omen in Filipino superstition. Cited in early chapters as a celestial echo during the author's birth. A thread of myth and mysticism tied to origin stories.

Harbour Bridge *(Australia)* – Sydney's iconic steel arch bridge spanning Port Jackson.

Harry Potter *(United Kingdom)* – Fantasy series by J.K. Rowling. Referenced as formative fiction that framed magic, identity, and belonging.

Harutan *(Philippines)* – Playful teasing or flirty banter. Captures the cultural lightness of Filipino friendships and romantic interactions. A way of bonding without pressure.

Harvard Law *(United States)* – One of the most prestigious law schools in the world. Symbol of academic aspiration.

Hauptbahnhof *(Germany)* – "Main train station." Common across German cities. Appears as a place of arrival, movement, and unexpected reflection. The architectural heart of German transit.

Haymarket *(Australia)* – Inner-city Sydney suburb known for markets and Chinatown.

Heaphy Track *(New Zealand)* – One of New Zealand's Great Walks, stretching through lush rainforests, alpine tussocks, and wild west coast beaches. Referenced as the trail that tested both body and resolve, but offered presence, perseverance, and ancestral quiet in return.

Hearty *(Proper name)* – Another sister who helped host the wake. Referenced in tandem with Nene as part of the family's gentle infrastructure of care.

Heidelberg *(Germany)* – Historic university city on the Neckar River. Scene of reflective walks.

Hemingway, Ernest *(Proper name)* – American writer of "A Moveable Feast", symbolizing self-discovery through foreign cities.

High Court *(Australia)* – The supreme court of Australia, often referenced to convey the stakes of constitutional law.

Hudson Valley *(United States)* – A scenic region north of New York City known for riverside towns, nature, and sophistication. Referenced as a place of reflection and whispering ambition during a road trip across the U.S.

Hunger Games *(United States)* – Dystopian trilogy by Suzanne Collins. Referenced metaphorically in reflections on law school stress and survival.

Hygge *(Denmark)* – A Danish concept of warmth, comfort, and joy. Referenced as a way of making meaning out of moments.

ICU (Intensive Care Unit) *(Global/Medical)* – A specialized hospital department providing critical care for patients with life-threatening conditions. Referenced often as part of the author's dual identity — the nurse trained in precision and presence. The backdrop of both exhaustion and resilience.

Idemo! *(Croatia/Serbia)* – "Let's go!" A phrase of shared action and energy. Part of Chapter 9's multilingual symphony of encouragement. Each version of "let's go" adds to the global chorus of persistence.

I Know Why the Caged Bird Sings *(United States)* – Autobiography by Maya Angelou about identity, trauma, and resilience. Acknowledged as a literary North Star for storytelling and truth-telling.

Ilongga *(Philippines)* – A woman from Iloilo province. Used to describe regional identity and affection in conversations about heritage and interpersonal connections.

Instagram *(Social media)* – A photo and video-sharing app popular for its aesthetic curation, filters, and visual storytelling. Referenced to contrast the author's simple, chaotic childhood with the curated perfection often found in online storytelling.

IOU *(Global)* – Short for "I owe you." A handwritten or verbal promise to repay a debt, common in rural Philippines where cash is scarce but trust is abundant. Referenced in the context of yema sales and early entrepreneurial grit.

Ipanema *(Brazil)* – A Rio de Janeiro beach made famous by the song Girl from Ipanema. Referenced during Olympic volunteer days for its rhythm and sensual energy.

IT Park *(Philippines)* – A modern business and tech district in Cebu City, bustling with BPO offices, 24/7 cafés, and young professionals chasing global dreams on night shifts. Referenced as the place where ambition and adobo meet under neon lights and the hum of possibility.

Jiāyóu! (加油!) *(China)* – Literally "add oil!" Used as a cheer meaning "keep going" or "you got this!" Another entry in the international cheer lexicon in Vamos.

Joan *(Proper name)* – The author's best friend and travel companion through Europe. Referenced in memories from Barcelona to Berlin, and later in life as a foil for the author's tempo — thoughtful, anchored, and fiercely loyal.

Joan Sutherland Theatre *(Australia)* – The principal opera venue of the Sydney Opera House, named after the famed soprano. Referenced as a place of grandeur and grief, where the author wept not just for the story on stage, but for his own unfolding.

Joie de vivre *(France)* – "Joy of living." The art of savoring life, especially in ordinary moments. Appears to describe the small, beautiful defiant pleasures — the morning pastry, the walk by the Seine, the art of savoring.

Jolie, Angelina *(United States)* – Actress and humanitarian. Referenced in a moment of aspirational irony and cultural shorthand for global beauty.

Jollibee *(Philippines)* – The Philippines' beloved fast-food chain, known for sweet spaghetti and sentimental ads. More than a meal, it's memory, identity, and comfort wrapped in red and yellow nostalgia.

Judge Judy *(United States)* – Judith Sheindlin, former U.S. family court judge and long-time host of the reality courtroom series *Judge Judy*. Known for her sharp tongue, eye-rolls, and fast verdicts, she's often referenced when distinguishing real legal procedure from TV dramatics.

Juju *(Colloquial)* – A playful or spiritual term for energy, vibe, or emotional rhythm. Used informally in the memoir to describe mood, momentum, or personal magic as the internal fuel behind decisions, recovery, or motivation.

Kafka, Franz *(Proper name)* – Czech writer known for surrealism and alienation. Referenced to capture themes of bureaucracy and surreal discomfort.

Kahikatea *(New Zealand)* – New Zealand's tallest native tree. Symbol of resilience in Māori proverbs. Referenced metaphorically for strength and persistent change.

Kamote *(Philippines)* – Sweet potato, often eaten boiled or fried. A staple food in Filipino households, especially in rural communities. Symbol of simplicity, frugality, and humble strength.

Karaoke *(Japan/Philippines)* – From *kara* (empty) and *oke* (orchestra), karaoke means "empty orchestra". Music minus the lead vocals. In the Philippines, it's ritual. A neighborhood soundtrack, a family bonding tool, and a safe space for joy, grief, or Gloria Gaynor.

Karakia *(Māori)* – Traditional prayers or incantations used to bless gatherings or moments of transition. Appears during the New Zealand chapters, especially in palliative care. Invokes sacred stillness and cultural reverence.

Karlskirche *(Austria)* – St. Charles Church, a baroque masterpiece with a green dome and pond reflections. A sacred, architectural exhale in Vienna, where the author wandered in silence and wondered what sacredness could mean outside of religion.

Katniss *(Fictional)* – Protagonist of "The Hunger Games" series. Referenced as a metaphor for survival, rebellion, and unexpected strength.

Kaya mo 'yan! *(Philippines)* – "You can do it!" A common phrase of encouragement. A phrase of pure, earnest encouragement used often by teachers, nurses, and mothers. Appears in moments of self-doubt and support.

Kea *(New Zealand)* – Mischievous alpine parrot with a penchant for shiny things and boots. Referenced as fashion police of the bush, judging newcomers and their squeaky shoes.

Kepler Track *(New Zealand)* – One of the Great Walks. An alpine loop near Te Anau with golden tussock and howling wind. First real trail tackled where tears, windburn, and awe met on a mountaintop.

King Street *(Australia)* – A main road running through Newtown in Sydney. Referenced as the cultural artery where the author experienced food, community, and memories.

King's Landing *(Fictional)* – Capital of the Seven Kingdoms in Game of Thrones. Used metaphorically in pop culture comparisons.

Kiwi *(New Zealand)* – A nickname for New Zealanders, also a nocturnal flightless bird. Referenced as a cultural identity, it is humble, humorous, and fiercely practical.

K-pop *(Korea)* – Korean pop music genre known for catchy hooks and elaborate choreography. A thread of global pop culture influence.

Krankenversicherung *(Germany)* – Health insurance system in Germany. Referenced in moments of bureaucratic hilarity and culture shock.

Kris *(Proper name)* – The author's ICU mentor. Symbolizes professional initiation, steady guidance, and the kind of leadership that transforms fear into confidence.

Kuya *(Philippines)* – "Older brother" or respectful term for an older male. Used frequently in Filipino culture to denote respect and familiarity. Appears in conversations, memory scenes, and workplace camaraderie.

Lahug *(Philippines)* – A barangay in Cebu City known for its mix of residential calm and commercial activity. Home to both family homes and high-rise dreams. Referenced as the quieter sibling to IT Park, the place where the author found grounding before flight.

Laksa *(Malaysia/Singapore)* – A spicy noodle soup with coconut milk. Referenced as a comfort dish tied to homesickness and healing.

Larapinta Trail *(Australia)* – A 223-kilometre walking track through the West MacDonnell Ranges in Central Australia. Burnt-orange dust, ancient silence, ridgelines that whisper resilience. A reminder that stillness could be found even in the driest parts of becoming.

Latinx *(United States)* – A gender-neutral term for people of Latin American descent. Used to reflect evolving language around identity and inclusivity during the author's reflections on cultural navigation.

La Traviata *(Italy)* – A tragic opera by Giuseppe Verdi. Referenced as an emotional and cultural climax, where the weight of language, love, and loss transcended subtitles.

Law-oy *(Philippines)* – A light vegetable soup made with greens and flavored with fish or shrimp. Simple, nourishing, and usually home-cooked. Represents both literal and emotional sustenance in the author's childhood.

Lazada *(Philippines)* – An online shopping platform. Symbol of the pre-Grab era, where shipping delays and misplaced parcels were part of the adventure.

Lira *(Italy/Turkey)* – A former currency in Italy and current in Turkey. Referenced in scenes involving currency conversion and the shifting value of things.

LMI *(Australia)* – Lenders Mortgage Insurance. Referenced in discussions of finance and property.

Lord of the Flies *(United Kingdom)* – Novel about boys stranded on an island, descending into savagery. Referenced as a cautionary tale about systems and the loss of structure.

Lord of the Rings *(New Zealand)* – Fantasy epic by J.R.R. Tolkien, later adapted into films largely shot in New Zealand. Referenced during the Tongariro trek, with Mount Ngauruhoe standing in as Mount Doom. A mythic lens on personal challenge and transformation.

Luxmore Hut *(New Zealand)* – An alpine shelter on the Kepler Track. Windy, exposed, breathtaking. Where reflection came easy and safety arrived like an old friend.

Ma'am Sarah *(Proper name)* – A clinical instructor at San Pedro College known for her empathy and no-frills wisdom. Later became Dean of the College of Nursing. Referenced as a grounding presence during a pivotal moment of burnout.

Magpet *(Philippines)* – A municipality in Cotabato, Mindanao and the author's hometown. The author's hometown and his starting point geographically and emotionally.

Magpet National High School *(Philippines)* – A public secondary school in Magpet, Cotabato. The author's high school alma mater. A formative institution that shaped early discipline, ambition, and the first stirrings of what it means to strive.

Mahjong *(China/Philippines)* – Strategic tile-based game. Referenced in family gatherings as metaphor for luck, legacy, and loud declarations.

Maison de l'Île-de-France *(France)* – One of the international student residences at Cité Internationale Universitaire de Paris. The author's base during the early years in Europe.

Maison du Japon *(France/Japan)* – Japanese residence within Cité Internationale Universitaire de Paris. A place of residence marked by order and cultural crossover.

Makati *(Philippines)* – The Philippines' financial capital. Appears as the place where author first took the NCLEX.

Mallorca *(Spain)* – The largest of the Balearic Islands in Spain. Sun-soaked, serene, and home to Rafael Nadal, but also a metaphor for return, recalibration, and inner calm.

Malong *(Philippines)* – A traditional Filipino tubular cloth, often handwoven, used as a blanket, wrap, skirt, or versatile garment. Common in Mindanao and across the southern Philippines, it holds both cultural and personal significance.

Mamatay naman ako, magkaon ta lami *(Philippines)* – Visayan for "Well, if I'm going to die anyway, can we at least eat something delicious?" A darkly humorous phrase used in moments of fatigue and stress. Showcases the Filipino tendency to use food and humor as medicine.

Mamiss mo ako *(Philippines)* – Visayan for "Will you miss me?" A tender, emotionally charged question used in personal relationships which echoes longing and insecurity.

Manacor *(Spain)* – A town on the island of Mallorca. The hometown of Rafael Nadal and the location of his tennis academy. Referenced as a site of athletic pilgrimage and grounding.

Manang *(Philippines)* – A Filipino respectful title for an older woman. Appears in family and rural healthcare scenes and conveys both affection and hierarchy.

Mandarin *(Philippines)* – A citrus fruit commonly grown in Mindanao. Represents both economic livelihood and sensory memory tied to the landscape of the author's childhood.

Manhattan *(United States)* – New York City borough known for its skyline, culture, and finance district.

Man in the Arena *(United States/France)* – A famous passage from Roosevelt's 1910 speech *Citizenship in a Republic*, delivered at the Sorbonne in Paris. It celebrates those who step into the metaphorical "arena" to strive, risk failure, and act with courage, rather than standing safely on the sidelines as critics.

Māori *(New Zealand)* – The tangata whenua (people of the land) of Aotearoa. Referenced in rituals, whānau dynamics, and treaty principles that shaped an inclusive healthcare model.

Mara Clara *(Philippines)* – A long-running teleserye about identity, secrets, and class struggle. Referenced as part of the pop culture landscape that shaped the author's emotional vocabulary growing up.

Maraming salamat *(Philippines)* – Filipino for "Thank you very much." A formal expression of gratitude. Used throughout in moments of gratitude in hospitals, homes, and goodbyes.

Marang *(Philippines)* – A tropical fruit with soft flesh and strong aroma, native to Mindanao. Evoked as part of the rural sensory experience — sticky, delicious, and uniquely Filipino.

Marbury *(Legal)* – *Marbury v. Madison* (1803), the U.S. Supreme Court case that established judicial review, a cornerstone of constitutional law and a recurring character in every bar exam taker's nightmares. Referenced as a ghostly whisper during the NY Bar.

Martin, George RR *(Proper name)* – American novelist best known for "A Song of Ice and Fire." Referenced as a literary parallel to complex journeys and unexpected turns.

MasterChef Australia *(Australia)* – An Australian competitive cooking reality TV show where amateur and professional chefs compete in culinary challenges. Known for its inspiring contestant stories, high-pressure cook-offs, and a focus on creativity, skill, and resilience in the kitchen.

Meine liebe Deutschland *(Germany)* – "My dear Germany." The author's own phrasing, later corrected to "*mein liebes Deutschland.*" Reflects both linguistic vulnerability and the emotional resonance of place.

Melange *(Austria)* – A Viennese-style coffee made with espresso and frothy milk, often served with a glass of water. The drink of choice for afternoons and slower thinking. A little creamier than purpose, a little stronger than nostalgia.

Metro Manila *(Philippines)* – The chaotic, pulsating heart of the Philippines. Known for jeepneys, shopping malls, and traffic that tests both patience and faith. Referenced as the backdrop for early nursing life — full of grit, SkyFlakes, and stories whispered between shifts and smog.

MFA *(Global)* – Master of Fine Arts, often in creative writing. Mentioned here not as a measure of worth, but to name the bias that polish must come from pedigree and not from lived experience.

Milo powder *(Philippines/Asia-Pacific)* – A chocolate malt drink mix beloved across the Philippines, Australia, and New Zealand. In the memoir, it's a childhood relic consumed straight from the tin "like sand but sacred."

Mindanao *(Philippines)* – The second-largest island in the Philippines and home to diverse cultures and the author's roots. The author's ancestral and emotional homeland. Appears as both setting and symbol throughout the book.

Mon ami *(France)* – French for "My friend." Used playfully and ironically in a bureaucratic context. Used with ironic charm in a bureaucratic anecdote. Signals both familiarity and distance, a tone Paris often demands.

Monet, Claude *(Proper name)* – French Impressionist painter famous for works like Water Lilies. Referenced in art-related reflections.

Mount Apo *(Philippines)* – The highest mountain in the Philippines, standing at 2,954 meters. A potentially active stratovolcano located on the island of Mindanao, revered both for its biodiversity and its symbolic stature in local identity. Referenced as the green and looming backdrop to childhood in Gubatan.

Mount Ngauruhoe *(New Zealand)* – Volcanic peak, famously "Mount Doom" in The Lord of the Rings. Referenced as both cinematic and spiritual mountain walked around, but never just passed.

MPRE *(Legal)* – The Multistate Professional Responsibility Examination, a standardized test on legal ethics. Required by most U.S. states for bar admission. Referenced as part of the author's journey through American legal licensure.

MRT *(Philippines)* – Mass rapid transit railway. Crowded, erratic, often smells like ambition and body spray. Survived by nurses, students, and the deeply hopeful. Referenced as part of the early professional grind.

MS Word *(Global)* – Short for Microsoft Word, a word processing program used to draft documents. For the author, it served as a canvas for piecing together scattered insights and journal entries that eventually formed this memoir.

München *(Germany)* – German name for Munich, capital of Bavaria.

Munggo *(Philippines)* – A Filipino dish made with mung beans, often cooked during Lent or simple family meals. Appears in scenes of domestic memory or cultural grounding.

Musei Vaticani *(Italy/Vatican City)* – The Vatican Museums, home to some of the world's most significant art and religious relics, including Michelangelo's Sistine Chapel. Referenced during the Rome leg of the author's journey as a place of beauty, bureaucracy, and long lines.

Museum of Broken Relationships *(Croatia)* – A Zagreb museum exhibiting objects from ended relationships. Referenced as an unexpectedly comforting site of collective vulnerability.

Nabokov, Vladimir *(Proper name)* – Russian-American novelist known for Lolita and elegant, intricate prose. Referenced as a wink to literary tradition — admired, but not imitated.

Naj *(Proper name)* – A Muslim nurse-turned-lawyer. Referenced as a leader who doesn't boom, but beams. Symbolizes steady strength.

Nanay *(Philippines)* – Tagalog/Visayan for "Mother". A central figure in the memoir, Nanay, the author's mother, represents tenderness, sacrifice, discipline, and the legacy of care that shaped the author's journey.

NCLEX *(Medical)* – The U.S. nursing licensure exam. A defining milestone in the author's nursing career. Passed while balancing multiple time zones and professional demands.

Nene *(Proper name)* – A sister who brewed coffee for mourners during the family wake. Referenced as one of the anchors of grace and hospitality during grief.

Newtown *(Australia)* – A suburb in Sydney known for its eclectic, artsy vibe. Referenced as a symbol of creative freedom and belonging.

New York Bar *(Legal)* – The licensing authority and examination for attorneys in New York State. Referenced as a major milestone in the author's legal journey, symbolizing both rigor and identity.

New York Board of Law Examiners *(Legal)* – Licensing authority for New York State lawyers. Referenced as both barrier and badge in the journey toward U.S. legal admission.

Ngo hiong *(Philippines/China)* – A five-spice spring roll commonly found in Visayan street food. Used as a sensory anchor in food scenes.

Niagara Falls *(United States/Canada)* – A roaring natural wonder and an accidental post-bar spiritual retreat. Part mist, part metaphor, part emotional pressure-washer.

Nokia *(Finland)* – Telecommunications company once dominant in mobile phones. Nostalgic nod in tech-related anecdotes.

Noli Me Tangere *(Philippines)* – A seminal novel by Filipino nationalist José Rizal, written in Spanish in 1887. Referenced as a book that awakened not just a nation, but the author's own sense of courage and cultural identity.

Nonoy *(Philippines)* – A common nickname for boys. Used in childhood memories. Often invoked with tenderness or teasing affection.

Nora *(Proper name)* – The sister based in Virginia, U.S., with whom the author stayed during visits. Referenced as an emblem of family warmth, Costco adventures, and diasporic belonging.

Northern Star *(Celestial)* – Also known as Polaris. A fixed point of navigation in the northern hemisphere. Referenced as a symbol of bold, clear guidance, in contrast to the subtler Southern compass.

North Island *(New Zealand)* – One of New Zealand's two main islands. Setting for several outdoor and migration chapters.

Notes *(Global)* – A built-in note-taking app on Apple devices. Quick, convenient, and often chaotic, this is where many of the author's rawest thoughts landed, usually typed half-asleep, mid-flight, or post-shift.

Notion *(Global)* – A digital workspace used for organizing notes, tasks, and projects. Many of the author's early story fragments lived here before they became chapters.

Notre-Dame *(France)* – A Gothic cathedral in Paris, iconic and symbolic. Featured in the author's story as the backdrop to a poetic encounter with an ice cream maker who taught craftsmanship over commerce.

NPO *(Medical)* – "Nothing by mouth." A common hospital directive used in clinical settings. Referenced in nursing chapters to highlight the language of medicine and control.

Nurse John *(Proper name)* – Filipino-American nurse and viral content creator known for comedic skits about hospital life. His videos, often performed in exaggerated accents and scrubs, capture the chaos, resilience, and absurdity of nursing with humor and uncanny accuracy.

Obama, Michelle *(Proper name)* – Former U.S. First Lady. Quoted and referenced in several reflections on grounded power and excellence.

Odessa *(Proper name)* – A friend who joined an East Coast trip.

OFW *(Philippines)* – Overseas Filipino Worker. A Filipino citizen working abroad, often in caregiving, construction, or domestic work. A recurring identity throughout the memoir. Hardworking, sacrificial, and often invisible OFWs are shown as both national heroes and personal reference points.

Oh, T.E. *(Medical)* – Professor Teik Oh (Teik E. Oh) is a pioneering Australian-based intensive care specialist, widely recognized for his leadership in critical care medicine and for authoring the seminal textbook, *Oh's Intensive Care Manual.* Symbolic of the author's early ICU days — confusion, precision, and learning how to save lives with one hand on a textbook.

Okay lang ko *(Philippines)* – Filipino for "I'm okay." A phrase often used to deflect concern, sometimes genuine, sometimes armor. Appears in high-pressure moments of the narrative.

On Earth We're Briefly Gorgeous *(United States)* – A lyrical novel by Ocean Vuong, written as a letter from a son to his illiterate mother. Referenced as a book that undid the author emotionally and showed how broken language can still carry truth.

Oriental Bay *(New Zealand)* – Wellington's jewel of a waterfront. The author described post-shift fish and chips here, watching dolphins like exclamation marks written by the sea.

Osprey *(Brand)* – American outdoor gear company known for its durable hiking packs. Referenced as smug, sturdy, occasionally judgmental hiking companion.

Paella *(Spain)* – A traditional rice dish from Valencia, often cooked with seafood, saffron, and served in a wide shallow pan. Shared during travel chapters as a communal ritual of waiting, savoring, and gathering.

Palmerston North Hospital *(New Zealand)* – A major regional hospital in the Manawatū-Whanganui region, serving as a training ground and reality check for new nurses. Referenced as a place of both professional challenge and personal growth.

Pan de sal *(Philippines)* – Slightly sweet bread rolls, a nostalgic breakfast staple. Appears in childhood and hospital lunchbox scenes. Warm, soft, and emblematic of Filipino mornings.

Pandora's box *(Mythology)* – A source of endless trouble once opened.

Pangao-an *(Philippines)* – A barangay in Magpet, Cotabato. Part of the author's rural roots. Cited in early chapters to map out the author's home geography.

Pansit *(Philippines)* – Stir-fried noodles eaten during celebrations, often symbolizing long life (but can also mean having a busy shift in the hospital). Woven into family gatherings, fiestas, and workplace potlucks — noodles as blessing and baseline.

Panthéon *(France)* – Monument in Paris housing the remains of notable French figures. Visited during reflective walks in Paris chapters.

Pão de queijo *(Brazil)* – Brazilian cheese bread made with cassava flour, crisp on the outside and chewy inside. Often a comfort snack in Rio de Janeiro.

Para hindi ka magutom *(Philippines)* – Filipino/Visayan for "So you won't go hungry." A typical Filipino expression of care, often said while packing extra food. Represents love through preparedness.

Passeig de Gràcia *(Spain)* – A major boulevard in Barcelona, lined with boutiques and Gaudí architecture. Appears in the memoir's Europe chapters as a blend of beauty, modernism, and elegance.

Pastéis de nata *(Portugal)* – Creamy egg custard tarts with caramelized tops. Enjoyed during the Lisbon chapter. Sweet, warm, and symbolic of the delights that travel affords.

Pastil *(Philippines)* – Rice topped with shredded meat and wrapped in banana leaves. Street food from Mindanao, mentioned in scenes that evoke memory and place.

Pâtisserie *(France)* – A shop specializing in pastries and sweets. Symbolizes pleasure, finesse, and the small indulgences of French living.

Pavlova *(Australia/New Zealand)* – A meringue-based dessert with a crisp crust and soft interior, topped with fruit. Referenced as a cultural pride point and a playful Oceanic rivalry during the author's time in both countries.

PCR Test *(Medical)* – COVID-era diagnostic tool. Referenced briefly as a bureaucratic hurdle during pandemic-related travel narratives.

Pesos *(Philippines/Mexico/etc.)* – Currency in several countries including the Philippines. Referenced during reflections on remittances and economic migration.

Pier 39 *(United States of America)* – Touristy San Francisco pier with chowder and sea lions. The author captured its chaos and charm. A backdrop to reflection in a loud, lovable city.

Pierogi *(Poland)* – Dumplings filled with potato, cheese, or meat. Traditional comfort food. Mentioned in Krakow as one of many honest bites that fed wonder more than hunger.

Pinoy *(Philippines)* – Informal term for a Filipino person. Used in moments of solidarity, pride, and shared identity especially abroad.

Plato *(Proper name)* – An ancient Greek student of Socrates and teacher of Aristotle, known for exploring justice, politics, and metaphysics.

Poblacion *(Philippines)* – The town center or downtown area of a municipality. Sets the stage for many provincial chapters in Mindanao as the hub of everyday life.

Pope Francis *(Proper name)* – Head of the Catholic Church from 2013 to 2025. Mentioned in faith-related reflections.

Pope John Paul II *(Proper name)* – Head of the Catholic Church from 1978 to 2005, canonized as a saint in 2014.

Prefectures *(France)* – Administrative divisions similar to states or provinces. Used when navigating local bureaucracy abroad.

Proud ko nimo ba *(Philippines)* – Visayan for "I'm proud of you." Often said casually, but heavy with meaning. A rare expression of pride in a culture that praises more through action than words.

Pulpo *(Spain/Portugal)* – Octopus, often grilled. Referenced in Lisbon as part of a meal that marked slow pleasure and exploration.

Qahtani, Mohammed *(Saudi Arabia)* – 2015 Toastmasters World Champion. His speech "cracked something open" in the author's soul and was proof that words could rescue, not just persuade.

Rafael Nadal *(Spain)* – Tennis icon known for mental toughness, grit, and humility. Appears in a pivotal sports memory when the author was watching Nadal live in Melbourne. His signature cry, Vamos, becomes a philosophical thread in the memoir.

Rafa Nadal Academy *(Spain)* – A world-renowned tennis training center founded by Rafael Nadal in Manacor, Mallorca. Mentioned as both a physical place and a symbolic one, where discipline meets legacy.

Rambutan *(Philippines/Southeast Asia)* – A hairy red fruit with sweet flesh and cousin of the lychee. Appears in food descriptions and rural memories. Exotic, tactile, and sensorially rich.

Rechtsanwaltskammer *(Germany)* – Literally "lawyers' chamber", the German bar association. Appears in the Frankfurt chapter. Used humorously to highlight the author's linguistic struggle with German legal bureaucracy and as a mouthful that encapsulates red tape and cultural dissonance.

Res Ipsa Loquitur *(Legal)* – Latin for "the thing speaks for itself." A tort doctrine invoked when something goes so obviously wrong that negligence is assumed.

Riesling *(Germany)* – Light, aromatic white wine. Referenced in chapters on German summers and soft celebrations.

Riza *(Proper name)* – The sister whose home became the author's launchpad during Manila training. Mentioned in the context of 4-hour commutes, survival meals, and shared sacrifice.

Rizal, José *(Proper name)* – Filipino writer, ophthalmologist, and revolutionary. Executed by the Spanish in 1896. Revered for using literature as a peaceful form of resistance. Referenced as a symbol of dignity reclaimed through words.

Rod Laver Arena *(Australia)* – The centre court of the Australian Open in Melbourne. A temple of tennis intensity where legends are made and where the author heard "Vamos" reverberate like gospel.

Roland-Garros *(France)* – The iconic clay-court stadium in Paris that hosts the French Open, one of tennis's four Grand Slam tournaments. Named after a pioneering French aviator, it's where Rafael Nadal achieved a record 14 titles. Referenced as a pilgrimage site for tennis lovers and believers in relentless motion.

Rolex *(Global)* – Mentioned to contrast material status symbols with deeper values of worth and legacy.

Rollers Bakehouse *(Australia)* – A sunlit nook tucked behind the surf of Manly Beach, known for its cult-status croissants and minimalist cool. Where the author found pastries with integrity, coffee with punch. A place where ambition met butter and pauses felt earned.

Ronald *(Proper name)* – A former nurse turned mortgage broker. Referenced as a guide who translated the complex language of finance into something relatable for Filipino migrants.

Roosevelt, Theodore *(Proper name)* – The 26th president of the United States (1901–1909), known for his progressive policies, robust leadership style, and enduring speeches on courage and perseverance.

Rothenburg ob der Tauber *(Germany)* – Well-preserved medieval town in Bavaria, Germany.

Routeburn *(New Zealand)* – A trail that reads like a poem. Swing bridges, fog like a lullaby, rivers in harmony. Referenced as the trail where solitude began to feel like a gift.

Royal Brisbane and Women's Hospital *(Australia)* – One of the oldest and busiest hospitals in Queensland. Where the author learned to keep pace, improvise, and carve space for compassion in clinical chaos.

Rumi *(Persia)* – A 13th-century Sufi poet and mystic. Quoted in Chapter 11 as a turning point toward inner reflection: "When will you begin that long journey into yourself?"

Sachertorte *(Austria)* – A rich chocolate cake with a thin layer of apricot jam and glossy ganache. Iconic in Vienna, especially when eaten slowly with whipped cream and a side of self-reflection. Decadent restraint, forked one memory at a time.

Sagrada Família *(Spain)* – An iconic, still-unfinished basilica in Barcelona designed by Antoni Gaudí. Described as "devotion in delay", a sacred space built slowly, with intention and awe. A metaphor for identity still under construction.

Salamat *(Philippines)* – Tagalog for "Thank you." A foundational word of gratitude. Simple, sincere, and deeply Filipino.

Saligan *(Philippines)* – A student legal advocacy group in San Pedro College.

Sangria *(Spain)* – A fruity wine-based punch made with chopped fruit and sometimes brandy. Appears during European travel scenes. Represents warmth, laughter, and the flavor of nights when everything felt both light and layered.

San Pedro College *(Philippines)* – A Catholic nursing college in Davao City. Its halls echo with prayers, pressure, and the forging of compassion under stress.

Santiago, Miriam Defensor *(Proper name)* – A firebrand Filipino senator, international judge, and author, known for her razor-sharp wit, fearless rhetoric, and uncompromising stance on justice. Referenced as an emblem of brilliance and boldness.

Sartre, Jean-Paul *(Proper name)* – Philosopher and writer known for existentialism. Invoked in meditations on freedom, absurdity, and self-definition.

Savoir-faire *(France)* – The ability to act appropriately in social situations with poise and charm. Gained through navigating Parisian bureaucracy, metro systems, and moments of cultural friction.

Schnitzel *(Germany / Austria)* – Breaded, fried meat cutlet. Referenced as both culinary icon and metaphor for unapologetic indulgence.

Schönbrunn Palace *(Austria)* – Vienna's imperial estate. The author called it "opulence with perfect posture." A nod to grandeur, discipline, and the weight of empire.

Seine *(France)* – The river that flows through Paris. Appears often in literature and in the memoir as a site of reflection.

Seneca *(Proper name)* – Ancient Roman Stoic philosopher and statesman. Known for writings on tranquility, brevity of life, and the importance of self-mastery. Referenced in contrast to the chaos of modern ambition and as proof that old wisdom still fits in new lives.

Shantaram *(Australia / India)* – Novel based on the author's real-life escape and immersion into Bombay's underworld. Referenced in literary reflections on place, reinvention, and contradiction.

She Used to Be Mine *(United States)* – A song by Sara Bareilles from the Broadway musical Waitress, about a woman unraveling under the weight of duty and remembering the girl she used to be.

Sibug Elementary School *(Philippines)* – The author's primary school in Mindanao. Referenced as the foundational place where early ambitions were born.

Sinigang *(Philippines)* – A sour soup usually made with tamarind and vegetables. A comfort food of the Filipino soul. Tart, warm, and healing, it appears in homesick cravings and memory-rich meals.

Sisig *(Philippines)* – A sizzling dish made from chopped pig's face and liver, often served with calamansi. Street food royalty.

Sister Faustina *(Proper name)* – Polish nun whose visions inspired the Divine Mercy devotion.

SkyFlakes *(Philippines)* – A dry cracker brand sold in foil packs. The unofficial snack of broke students, tired nurses, and diasporic homes. A recurring motif of survival.

Snapper Rocks *(Australia)* – A world-class surf break near Coolangatta. For the author, it was saltwater therapy, where the roar of the ocean softened the noise of ambition.

SOAP notes *(Nursing)* – A standardized medical documentation format: Subjective, Objective, Assessment, Plan. The author joked about trying to make yours sound like House M.D. wrote them — drama, detail, and all.

Sorbonne *(France)* – Prestigious university in Paris, historically known for humanities and law. Referenced in the memoir as an emblem of intellectual pursuit and the complexity of studying abroad.

Southport *(Australia)* – A coastal suburb on the Gold Coast, Queensland, referenced in the context of the early experiences in Australia, highlighting its blend of residential and commercial areas.

Sprezzatura *(Italy)* – Italian for effortless style that conceals the effort behind it.

SSS *(Philippines)* – Social Security System, a government agency for worker benefits. Referenced to illustrate the bureaucratic realities of working Filipinos.

Starbucks / Coffee Bean *(Global)* – Coffee chains symbolic of urban aspiration and class comfort. Mentioned in the contrast between professional polish and personal exhaustion. Ritual spaces for working, hiding, and recharging.

Stoicism *(Ancient Philosophy)* – A school of philosophy that teaches virtue through reason, emotional regulation, and focus on what one can control. Referenced throughout as a personal compass, particularly in ICU chaos and legal detours.

STAT Page *(Medical)* – A rapid-response documentation tool in hospitals. Referenced during ICU scenes to emphasize urgency and life-or-death moments.

Streuselkuchen *(Germany)* – A crumb cake in Frankfurt, it becomes a tool for winning over colleagues. Sugar as diplomacy.

Survivor *(United States)* — A long-running reality show where strangers outwit, outplay, and outlast each other in tough conditions. Also known as immigrant life, minus the tribal council, but with just as much strategy and exhaustion.

Sydney Opera House *(Australia)* – Architectural icon and cultural heartbeat. Not just a tourist magnet, but a symbol of reinvention.

Sydney Symphony Orchestra *(Australia)* – One of the world's leading orchestras, based at the iconic Sydney Opera House. Referenced not just for its music, but for the moments when sound becomes story.

Table Topics *(Toastmasters)* – A segment where participants speak impromptu on a given topic for 1-2 minutes, referenced as part of the user's journey in Toastmasters, contributing to their development in public speaking and leadership.

Tagalog *(Philippines)* – One of the major languages of the Philippines, it is the basis for the national language, Filipino. Used throughout the memoir as a linguistic foundation, an identity marker, and a bridge between worlds.

Tallebudgera *(Australia)* – A calm, turquoise estuary in Queensland. In contrast to ICU chaos, the author called it a "reset button".

Tapas *(Spain)* – Small savory dishes, often shared with drinks. Appears in the memoir as a metaphor for conversation, community, and slow enjoyment. Dishes designed for staying, not rushing.

Tatay *(Philippines)* – Tagalog/Visayan term for "father". Used to describe the author's hardworking father whose love was shown through labor, not words.

Teleserye *(Philippines)* – A television drama series. Emotional backbone of Filipino pop culture. Referenced to describe emotional endurance, melodrama, and long-form storytelling.

The Alchemist *(Brazil)* – A fable about following one's dreams. Referenced to contextualize search for meaning during travel.

The Barber of Seville *(Italy)* – A comic opera by Gioachino Rossini. Referenced as an unexpectedly joyful escape into music and mischief and proof that even serious people need silliness sometimes.

The Year of Magical Thinking *(United States)* – Memoir by Joan Didion about grief and mourning. Listed among literary influences that shaped the memoir's tone and intent.

Three Bs *(Germany)* – A musical shorthand for Germany's classical heavyweights: Bach, Beethoven, and Brahms. Evoked in the memoir during an orchestral performance, representing not just legacy but emotional lineage. The composers whose notes still hold.

TikTok *(Social media)* – Short-form video platform. Referenced as a symbol of a world addicted to noise, scrolls, and spectacle.

Tine *(Philippines)* – A nickname, often short for Kristine or Christine. Used in the memoir for warmth and familiarity.

Toastmasters *(Global)* – A nonprofit focused on communication and leadership skills. In the memoir, it becomes a place of voice-finding and reinvention.

Toastmasters World Conference *(Global)* – The author's sacred pilgrimage of storytelling. A place "where small talk was performance art and healing hid in the applause."

Tolkien / The Hobbit *(New Zealand)* – Reference to the Wellington film premiere. Symbolizes whimsy, cultural immersion, and finding magic in unexpected places.

Tolkien, JRR *(Proper name)* – John Ronald Reuel Tolkien. English author of The Lord of the Rings. Used metaphorically when describing adventures, epic journeys, or identity quests.

Tongariro Northern Circuit *(New Zealand)* – Volcanic terrain with a side of sulfur. Home to Mount Ngauruhoe and moonlike landscapes. Referenced as mythological terrain and metaphor for internal transformation.

Toto *(Philippines/Proper name)* – A common nickname for boys in the Visayas and Mindanao, often used with tenderness. Referenced as the author's brother who braved childhood treks and carried paternal weight early on.

Tort *(Legal)* – A foundational subject in common law. Referenced in law school chapters as both rite of passage and academic torment.

Treaty of Waitangi *(New Zealand)* – A foundational document signed in 1840 between the British Crown and various Māori chiefs. It established British law in New Zealand while (theoretically) affirming Māori rights, though interpretations have long been contested. Represents law as living history full of complexity, contradiction, and contested justice.

Trotsky, Leon *(Proper name)* – A Russian-Austrian revolutionary thinker and exile who once sat in Viennese cafés between revolutions. Mentioned in proximity to Café Central, his presence haunting the margins of ambition, ideology, and exile.

Tsismis *(Philippines)* – Tagalog for gossip. Often dismissed, but also a source of community bonding, humor, and oral tradition. Appears in break rooms, barbershops, and barangays. More than rumor, it's a form of social survival and collective storytelling.

Tui *(New Zealand)* – A native bird with iridescent feathers and complex songs. Referenced as a chorus leader in early trail mornings, singing travelers awake.

Twitter *(Social media)* – A microblogging platform turned cultural battlefield where thoughts are condensed into 280 characters and outrage gets better engagement than nuance. Referenced in the question of whether ancient philosophers could survive modern algorithms.

USCIS *(United States)* – United States Citizenship and Immigration Services. The federal agency that processes immigration applications and petitions. Referenced frequently in legal and immigration chapters as a central institution in the author's work and clients' journeys.

Uluru *(Australia)* – A massive sandstone monolith in the Northern Territory sacred to the Anangu people. Referenced as a tourist site and a breathing presence — ancient, unmoved, and holding stories older than colonization.

Utang na Loob *(Philippines)* – A deep sense of debt of gratitude in Filipino culture, often toward family or mentors. Explored as a moral and emotional inheritance shaping personal decisions.

Van Gogh, Vincent *(The Netherlands)* – Dutch post-impressionist painter known for his emotional intensity and tragic life. A figure of misunderstood brilliance and beauty born from fracture. Patron saint of those who feel deeply and try anyway.

Visayan *(Philippines)* – Refers to both the people and languages from the Visayas region of the Philippines, including Cebuano, Hiligaynon, and Waray. A crucial layer of the author's identity. Visayan culture and dialect inform the memoir's rhythm, worldview, and humor.

Vivaldi, Antonio *(Proper name)* – Italian-Austrian composer of The Four Seasons and patron saint of violins that ache like memory. Referenced as a musical companion in Europe, his music often cueing introspection, movement, or both.

Vltava River *(Czech Republic)* – The longest river in the Czech Republic. Charles Bridge crosses it. Described as spellbound with music and memory in Prague.

Volé *(France)* – French for "stolen." Used after a street theft in Paris. Represents the literal and metaphorical moments of loss and letting go.

Voltaire *(Proper name)* – French enlightenment writer and philosopher. Referenced indirectly in the philosophical undertones of the author's Paris musings.

Vuong, Ocean *(Proper name)* – Vietnamese-American poet, essayist, and novelist known for his lyrical, soul-baring work on identity, grief, love, and survival. Quoted as a literary touchstone for tenderness that dares to persist.

Waitress *(United States)* – A Broadway musical by Sara Bareilles about Jenna, a pie-making waitress who learns to choose herself. It becomes a metaphor for transformation and a proof that even ordinary lives can hold revolutionary acts.

Wall Street *(United States)* – Financial district in Lower Manhattan, symbolic of ambition and capitalism.

Watsons Bay *(Australia)* – A harborside village in Sydney. Referenced during moments of solitude and the tension between luxury and loneliness.

Wawrinka, Stan *(Proper name)* – A Swiss Grand Slam champion and former top 5 player known for his punishing backhand and explosive performance under pressure. Defeated Nadal in the 2014 Australian Open final.

Weka *(New Zealand)* – Flightless bird with a curious temperament and dinosaur-like gait. Referenced as a mistaken velociraptor and reluctant passport recipient.

Weena Bus *(Philippines)* – A long-distance bus company in Mindanao. Referenced as part of early commutes, marking the physical and emotional distance between ambition and home.

Wellington Regional Hospital *(New Zealand)* – The author's first ICU post in New Zealand. Perched on a hill, often shrouded in wind and sea mist, it smelled of coffee, chlorhexidine, and courage. A place where the author learned to hold the line between life and loss.

West Coast *(United States)* – Western seaboard of the United States. Setting for travel and cultural contrasts.

Western Union *(Global)* – A financial services company used for sending money internationally. Referenced in the context of supporting family while working abroad.

Whānau *(Māori)* – Extended family or community of related people. In Māori culture, whānau goes beyond biological ties, it reflects kinship, care, and collective identity. Used to describe the relational warmth and interdependence.

Wieliczka Salt Mine *(Poland)* – A historic underground salt mine near Kraków, famous for its labyrinthine tunnels, saline lakes, and intricate chapels carved entirely out of salt. Referenced as a metaphor for hidden beauty, endurance, and the sacred spaces built deep within hardship.

Wiener Schnitzel *(Austria)* – Veal-based national dish of Austria. Referenced in Vienna chapter for its dramatic size and symbolic comfort.

Wilde, Oscar *(Proper name)* – Irish playwright and wit, author of The Picture of Dorian Gray. Patron saint of wit and rebellion. Quoted in the humor chapter: "Life is too important to be taken seriously." Wilde's irreverence complements the author's playful resilience.

Willkommen *(Germany)* – German for "welcome." Used in both sincerity and irony in German chapters.

World Championship of Public Speaking *(Global)* – The Olympics of oratory. The author watched it as a believer that speeches can become soul sport.

World Youth Day *(Global)* – A gathering of young people from around the world to celebrate faith and solidarity. Referenced in the "100 Days of Summer" chapter. A moment of spiritual reconnection and international camaraderie.

WTA (Women's Tennis Association) *(Global)* – The principal organizing body of women's professional tennis. Mentioned in connection with Alexa Eala's rise. Represents global recognition and the breaking of barriers for Filipina athletes.

Wunderbar *(Germany)* – German for "wonderful." Used with irony or affection throughout the German chapters.

Yema *(Philippines)* – A soft, sweet candy made from condensed milk and egg yolks. Wrapped in colorful cellophane and passed around classrooms and bus rides. Nostalgic and homemade, it is a taste of Filipino childhood.

Zoom *(Global)* – Video conferencing platform that became a lifeline for remote work and connection during the COVID-19 pandemic.

7-Eleven *(Global)* – A global convenience store chain. Referenced as a symbol of urban familiarity and late-night survival food.

About the Author:

Novie Onor is a Philippine-born and raised, Australian-educated, Europe-seasoned, New York-qualified lawyer, and a multijurisdictional ICU nurse who knows how to hold both a legal brief and a grieving hand.

He has lived many lives in one: a village child chasing fireflies in Mindanao, a migrant nurse navigating shiftwork and longing, a law scholar in Paris translating both French and ambition. Today, he stands at the intersection of healing and justice, having founded a global immigration law firm devoted to honoring stories in motion.

Novie writes the way he lives, with equal parts soul and strategy, humor and heart. Whether in nursing, in law, or on the page, his work is always about bearing witness to courage and offering clarity where there's fog.

He currently lives in Sydney, Australia (and soon, Springfield, Oregon) and somewhere between memory and momentum.

This is his first book.
He will write many more.

To the readers who made space in their hearts and shelves for this memoir — thank you.

This memoir was written across airports and hospital corridors, in the calm between immigration case files and ICU shifts, and in the fragile hours where grief and hope held hands.

If you've made it to this page, you've journeyed with me — through countries, careers, and the messy magic of establishing identity, choosing courage, and eventually, becoming.

To my family: you are the heartbeat beneath every word.

To Nanay: this is your story, too. I carried you in every sentence.

To my mentors, colleagues, and friends across borders — thank you for seeing me before I fully saw myself.

And to the dreamers, immigrants, caregivers, and quietly brave souls:

May these pages remind you that your story matters. That your identity is valid. And that the path to becoming is rarely straight, but always sacred.

Maraming salamat. Xie xie. Shukriya. Merci. Danke. Grazie.
Thank you.

Let's keep going — *Vamos!*